The Fairhaven Series

Destiny Lives on FAIRHAVEN STREET

A Father's Memoir of
First Love, Sacrifice and Perseverance

C.J. HUDSON

Black Rose Writing | Texas

©2023 by C.J. Hudson
All rights reserved. No part of this book may be reproduced, stored in a retrieval system or transmitted in any form or by any means without the prior written permission of the publishers, except by a reviewer who may quote brief passages in a review to be printed in a newspaper, magazine or journal.

The author grants the final approval for this literary material.

First printing

Some names and identifying details have been changed to protect the privacy of individuals.
ISBN: 978-1-68513-305-4
PUBLISHED BY BLACK ROSE WRITING
www.blackrosewriting.com

Printed in the United States of America
Suggested Retail Price (SRP) $20.95

Destiny Lives on Fairhaven Street is printed in Minion Pro

*As a planet-friendly publisher, Black Rose Writing does its best to eliminate unnecessary waste to reduce paper usage and energy costs, while never compromising the reading experience. As a result, the final word count vs. page count may not meet common expectations.

Praise for
Destiny Lives on Fairhaven Street

Awards won by *Destiny Lives on Fairhaven Street* as of January 2023
Literary Titan Silver Award (June 2022)
Literary Titan Gold Award (December 2022)
Best Book Award 2022 Cross Genre Novel - Finalist
Reader's Choice for Best Adult Book (November 2022) - Finalist
Firebird Book Awards, Best Inspirational Novel (July 2022)
Firebird Book Awards, Best Romantic Suspense Novel (July 2022)
2022 Hollywood Book Festival, Best Unpublished Novel - Runner Up
2022 International Impact Book Award - Best Inspirational Novel
2022 New York Book Festival, Best Unpublished Novel - Runner Up
2022 New York Book Festival, Best Memoir - Honorable Mention
2022 Best Thriller Book Award, Best Romantic Suspense - Finalist
Pinnacle Book Achievement Award - Fall 2022

Reviews

"If you only read one book this year, let it be this one."
–**N.N. Light's Book Heaven**

"*Destiny Lives on Fairhaven Street* is a captivating and motivating memoir that will push its readers to believe in three things—love, fate, and hope." –***Literary Titan***

"…a story so powerful that even the most cynical reader will walk away thinking about the book's themes long after the last page is read."
–***Onlinebookclub.com***

"An exceptional emotional read."
–***The Reading Bud***

"Hudson transcends the darkness and captures with shining clarity what it means to find and express true love."
–***Indies Today***

"The ending of this story brings an unexpected and shocking revelation regarding his relationship with Danielle."
–***Blueink Review***

To my sons, Maximus and Collin, my magnum opuses. This is the story of how you came to be. This is also who your father is, for good and for bad. Of all the things I've accomplished in my life, the two of you are by far the greatest. Always know that your mom and I love you both so very much and are so proud of the boys you are and the men we know you will become. I can think of no two better men to carry on my legacy. Never be afraid to love, for love is the most powerful force in existence. Let my life remind you of the most important lesson I can teach you: the man each of you is destined to become is the one you choose to be.

—Your father

To Cassandra Pereira: the Bernie to my Elton. One of the absolute best editors out there. You helped me find my written voice and were one of the few people who truly understood just how deep 35-year-old love can go. Our friendship was unexpected fruit from the tree of my story. Buckle up, because our best work is yet to come.

Destiny Lives on Fairhaven Street

This book is a memoir written about actual events, though names have been changed or omitted to ensure privacy. It presents the events depicted within to the best of the author's recollection. Contained within are graphic depictions of domestic violence and adult language. For those sensitive to such things, this book will be upsetting. For those brave enough to face these upsetting realities, you are about to read how love can conquer all things.

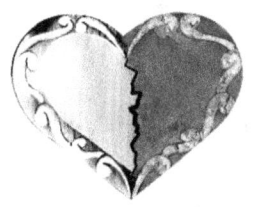

1

"I'm Just a Kid"
(by Simple Plan)

Your father wasn't always as you know him today. I wasn't always strong enough to pick each of you up with one arm and toss you across the couch. I wasn't always brave enough to say what was on my mind. I wasn't always confident enough to stand up to anyone who stepped out of line. Back when I was your age, I was none of those things and my classmates all knew this.

In school I asked to be called Chris, but everyone taunted me with the nickname my father gave me: C.J. As far back as I can remember, I hated the name C.J. My skin would crawl every time I heard it. But back then, I couldn't do anything to stop them.

I didn't look as you might imagine I did, either. Though I'm tall and strong now, my shoulders were narrow back then. My face was bony, with large ears that stuck out from each side of my head. When I took my shirt off, you could see almost every rib in my chest. I wore thick, black glasses. My teeth leaned inward in my upper jaw except for the two in front, which stuck out in an overbite. When I was tired, my left eye would face inward toward my nose. My hazel eyes shifted between brown when I was upset and green when I was happy. Back then, they weren't green very often.

I was a loner, and not by choice. Girls wanted absolutely nothing to do with me, shrieking in terror and running away when I would try to talk to them. Those who stuck around would pretend to like me, only to suddenly say they would never like anyone who looked like I did. One even gave me a valentine with a caricature of me hanging from a noose.

I was every bully's favorite target. The worst of them were stuck together in a group of four. They used to hang out in the school cafeteria and force me to pay a toll to eat. Tom, their leader, towered over me, a scraggly beanpole of red hair and ill intent.

"You know the drill, C.J. Your lunch money, or else." This was his usual bark as he pounded a fist into his palm. His oversized metal smile leaked the repugnant smell of garlic and sauerkraut left out in the trash.

"I can't eat if I don't have any money," I replied, voice lowered, eyes downward.

"That's your problem," he retorted. "Give it to us, or we'll pound you into the ground!"

Out of habit, I pulled out the $2.50 I had in my pocket. He snatched it from my hand before I could even offer it, shoving me hard into a nearby table. The four of them roared with laughter as I stumbled away, clutching my hip as I hobbled along. I sat alone down at the far end of the last table and watched everyone else eat.

Some days Tom's gang would pat me down like I was being arrested, joyfully describing the unspeakable things they would do to me if I dared to arrive empty-handed. I looked at the adults stationed nearby, supposedly there to protect me. They were absorbed in their own little world, backs turned and chatting enthusiastically among themselves. Only once did they notice me, and that resulted in a call to my mother to inform her I was not eating lunch.

I lied and said I had lost my lunch money, afraid of what my father would do to me if he knew I was getting bullied. My father despised weakness. No one coming from his loins would allow himself to get picked on, and if it happened, there'd be consequences. His punishments all began the same: with the unbuckling of his belt and the hiss of leather sliding off corduroy.

But my mother covered for me. She knew he would want his money back if I wasn't eating. Since I'd have no money to give back, he would assume that I'd spent it. If I dared to spend it in ways other than what it was intended for, it was stealing, at least in my father's eyes. He used to laugh every time he told us the story of how he put his best friend in the hospital for taking money from his wallet, like it was a crowning achievement in his life.

Mom suggested to my father that she should take overpaying for my lunches since he worked so hard for his money. This worked for a while until one day when she was running late for work and forgot to give me the money. By the time I realized it, it was too late.

All day I dreaded what would happen at lunch. I thought about hiding in the bathroom, but the adults kept a head count. They led me in that day like a lamb to the slaughter.

Tom's fiendish grin greeted me. It was payday. I assumed the position, and he waited as I searched my pockets for money that wasn't there. Growing impatient, he thrust his own hands into my pockets, violently moving them around.

"What the hell, C.J.? You holding out on us?"

"My parents didn't give me any money today."

He ripped his hands back out of my pockets and brought his face within an inch of my own. His breath was especially bad that day.

"You know what happens now, don't ya?"

I swallowed hard and avoided eye contact as he waited for an answer. His face suddenly shifted back to that horrible grin as I remained silent. I looked to my right shoulder, feeling his hand rest upon it. He nodded to the other three, who came in close, shielding us from any prying adult eyes.

"It's okay," he said calmly. "I'm gonna cut you a break this time. Looks like someone got to you before I could, anyway. Did someone hurt you?"

I slowly nodded; my head pointed down.

This guy is going to kill you.

"Your parents hit you at home?"

Again, I nodded. Tom clicked his tongue.

"I'm sorry to hear that, man. It's okay."

I slowly looked up at him. He seemed genuine. Maybe this would not be so bad after all. He nodded as he smiled at me. I felt my defenses draw down.

I suddenly crumbled to my knees, wheezing and gasping for air. He had hit me in the stomach so fast I didn't see it coming. I found myself pushed to the ground as he began stomping me in the stomach and ribs. One of his friends gleefully joined him as the other two played lookout. Instinctively, I curled into a ball to protect myself.

"Teacher! Teacher!" the lookouts yelled after a long minute or two. The four of them scattered as I lay there coughing, bleeding, and shivering. I slowly looked up as two sets of adult feet hurried into view.

They took me to the school nurse, who held an ice pack over my severely beaten face. The principal joined the room, and they demanded that I tell them who did this to me. I knew better than to tell them. The only thing that could make my situation worse than non-compliance was being a tattletale. They grilled me for information but eventually gave up.

"Okay then," the principal huffed, "we're going to have to notify your parents."

The heat of my face suddenly drained ice cold. No way could they tell my parents I was fighting at school! My father had a simple rule when it came to fighting: you better win. If you lost, he'd beat you as well.

"Please, please don't call them," I pleaded. "My mom is at work and my dad will kill me!"

"If you don't want me to call him, then tell me who beat you up, C.J."

"Please don't call me that," I said in a whisper. He had to lean in so he could hear me.

"Why not? That's your name, isn't it?"

"My name is Chris."

"Who did this to you?" he repeated slowly. Still, I said nothing. He shook his head and went into his office next door. He looked at me one last time as he picked up the phone to dial. I studied his expression as he waited, his shoulder pressing the phone to his head as he waited for an answer. I could hear nothing through the sealed cocoon of his office.

Please, let him be passed out.

The principal's mouth began moving on the other side of the glass window. We didn't have an answering machine, so that meant only one thing. As the moments passed, I saw his face shift. What had begun as a neutral expression suddenly switched to discomfort. Within moments, he had gone completely silent.

He looked up at me again, his grip loosening on the phone as he continued to listen. I knew that look. It was the same look of shock and pity that I had received from adults before when they met my dad. He slowly hung up and made his way out to the hallway. "Um… go back to class, young man," he said, shaken.

I was done. He knew I was done. He didn't even know my father that well, and he knew I was done. As I opened the door to the hallway, he called out to me one last time.

"Try to have a good rest of the day, okay, Chris?"

Back in class, it was difficult to focus when I knew the proverbial shit had hit the fan. My schoolwork was already subpar because I thought I was too stupid to keep up with everyone else, an accusation I'd grown accustomed to at school and at home. I buried my face in my arms, wishing I could just disappear.

Your great-grandmother, the only person who ever felt like an ally to me back in those days, would always tell me, "If you don't like something, pray about it!" I didn't really believe in God. The whole idea of a benevolent being didn't line up with my life experience up to that point. But at that moment, I was desperate.

I prayed that one day I would meet someone who would love me. Just one person who would care about me and not judge me for the way I looked. I begged God to not be lonely anymore. Even with my ribs still burning, the sting of loneliness hurt worst of all. They say no matter how hard or strange something is, you get used to it after a while. That is a lie.

I dismissed the whole thing after I was done. No way was praying to some magical being going to solve my problems. I never would've believed that, in a few short years, my prayer would be answered in what would become one of the most beautiful moments in my life. That moment would eventually lead to your dad becoming the man you know today. But we weren't there…not yet.

The thick Florida heat bore down on me as I made my way off school property that afternoon. The mosquitoes were out early, following me as I walked home covered in the scent of my own blood. As I got closer to our house, an all-too-familiar sense of terror crept up my spine.

Truth was, I wasn't scared of getting beat up. This lack of fear wasn't out of some sense of bravery, but because I had become used to it. Your uncle Scott and I frequently showed up at school with bruises on us, the product of "falling downstairs" (though our house only had one floor), "hitting walls" and "brotherly dispute." Back in the '80s, there weren't the same stringent laws protecting children from violence as there are now. Adults might have asked what happened if you came in with injuries but didn't press any further if you had a reasonable excuse.

I knew my father was getting his belt ready. Oddly enough, his aim seemed to improve when he was inebriated. No doubt he would lose control in a fit of rage. I humiliated him because the school had to call him. Scott had learned the repercussions of such a thing before. As I neared the front door to our house, I stopped for a moment to take a deep breath.

A small part of me held out hope. It all came down to what kind of mood he was in. Was he in a good mood? A bad mood? And how drunk? If he was in a good mood, and only a little drunk, then we might get through the night. But as every beating got progressively worse, I feared the day would come when he would kill one of us. Since I was the smallest, I figured I was the primary candidate.

I heard yelling from the other side of the door as I quietly crept up to our house.

"I'll kill him as soon as he walks in that door!"

"John, you need to calm down right now," she sternly replied.

"Shut the hell up! You lied to me too! I'll deal with you after I'm done with him!"

Even at such a young age, I somehow knew that night was going to be significant. Going through that door would begin a chain of events that would change the course of our family forever. That life of violence that I grew up with had plagued our family for almost one hundred years and three generations before me. Getting through that night would mark the beginning of its end. But I had to open that door so the night could begin, a night that would end with an ambulance in our driveway.

"Where the hell is C.J.?" he yelled. "It's already dark!"

God, I really hate that name.

This had to be done. Taking a deep breath, I slowly pushed the door open. My head jerked backward as I was yanked inside, the door swallowing me as it shut.

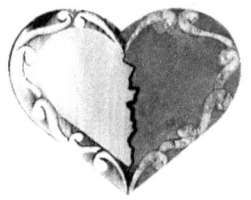

2

"Objects In the Rear-View Mirror May Appear Closer Than They Are"
(by Meatloaf)

A searing pain shot down my right arm. My father's nails dug into my skin as he sent me sailing inside. As violently as he'd pulled me into the house, the nearby wall causing the sudden arrest of my momentum was just as jarring.

I could feel his breath on the top of my head as he looked at me, hot with the familiar smell of beer and Pall Mall cigarettes. I kept my gaze at his midsection, obedient to another of his rules: no eye contact. Even today, with all my confidence, sometimes I have to remind myself to look others in the eye.

Beer cans were all over the living room floor. Some were upright, some tipped over and dripping onto the spotted brown carpet. The majority were around a patched-up La-Z-Boy that he frequently passed out in. Our living room smelled like the back end of a brewery during a heatwave.

Nearer to my face was his fist, balled tight by his side, his other hand gripping his folded, fake leather belt. The curled end hung low and swung gently as he shifted his weight. I kept my eyes on it, waiting for it to shoot up, which gave me the signal to brace myself. But my peripheral vision picked up a figure hastily moving toward us from the kitchen as well. My mother must have heard my entrance. She rushed to my father's side and began trying to put herself between us. She knew he beat us, but he never did it in front of her, so she could pretend she didn't know. Her children were naturally clumsy, at least according to him.

This was the first time I had ever seen her stand up to him.

"Don't you dare do what I think you're going to do!"

He shoved her away, but she caught herself before falling.

"Get off me, woman! I'm dealing with something here," he growled, returning his attention to me.

"I spoke with your principal today," he slurred. "He told me you haven't been eating lunch for a while now. But up till a couple of weeks ago, I've been giving you lunch money to feed your ass. Correct?"

I quickly nodded.

"But he says you weren't eating. So where's my money?"

I was too scared to speak. He loomed over me, waiting for an opportunity to pounce. That's how these things went. I either got hit for saying the wrong thing, or I got hit for saying nothing at all. He gritted his teeth together as he spoke.

"Boy, you know what happens if you don't answer me."

"It... some kids took it from me."

The tension in the room grew thicker. I kept my head down. He reached down and pulled my face up so he could inspect me. My gaze immediately shot to the wall near me.

"It looks like they kicked your ass."

I nodded. Back in those days, I was still young enough to hope for sympathy, though I knew better. He drew in a deep breath.

"I know for damn sure you didn't win. Did you at least fight back?"

Reluctantly, I shook my head no.

"So let me get this straight," he said, tapping his belt against his thigh. "Not only did you get your ass kicked, but you were also a loser who didn't fight back. On toppa that, you've been taking MY money day in and day out while lying to me! So that makes you a loser and a liar."

He was getting angrier by the syllable.

"Yep. A loser, a liar, and a thief. Now, I've told you before what happens to people who steal from me. Nobody steals from me, understood?"

I continued nodding in downcast silence.

The small blond mustache that covered his top lip curled downward as he studied me. His cold, brown eyes slowly closed.

"Hold out your arm. You have school tomorrow so you can wear a long-sleeved shirt," he said coldly.

I hesitated. At least it would be on the arm this time. There were no set number of lashes. He usually struck until he got tired. Last time my back was purple for a week. For my hesitancy, he snatched a handful of my hair with one hand. The next minute, I was down on all fours. My jaw felt like there was acid on it.

My mother screamed. From the floor, I saw her feet scurry toward my father's. They started struggling, almost grappling.

I don't quite remember what happened from that moment on, but eventually my mother hit the floor next to me. As soon as she landed, she crawled on top of me, covering me with her body and clutching me in her arms. Her entire body tensed as she held my small body under her. She was using herself as a shield.

"If you think you're gonna hit my baby again, you're going to have to kill me first!"

He loomed over us, the belt still clenched tightly in his hand, but he didn't strike. Noticing his sudden pause, she softly told me to go to my room.

"NO!" he belted out. "You go sit on the couch. You can watch what happens when someone mouths off to me."

My mother screamed and cried against it, but my father's mind was made up. "Either he sits on the couch to watch you take the beating he deserves, or I'll beat him till he stops breathing. Your choice."

She sobbed, her body heaving on top of mine, but only for a moment. Perhaps realizing we had no choice, she quietly told me to go to the couch as she stood up. Reluctantly, I did as I was told. My shirt was accumulating water spots from my tears.

"Now you watch close…" my father said, pointing the belt at me. "Actions have consequences. You know the consequences of stealing from me, but since your mom chose to take your punishment for you, all you have to do is watch. How noble of her."

He punched her so hard she spun around like a drunken ballerina before crashing to the floor.

"See her? This happens when you don't fight back."

She screamed as he kicked her with his steel-toed boot.

She brought her arms to hide her face as her husband whipped the belt over her, over and over. The first hit rolled her over, the second and third put her into a fetal position.

He hammered her repeatedly, first in the ribs, since her arms covered her face. He then struck her head five more times after her arms dropped to protect her side. Each facial strike landed worse than the next. Her blood splattered onto the carpet and the couch where I sat.

"Stupid fucking…" he repeated with each blow. Eventually, her arms dropped to the floor, rendering her completely defenseless.

He's going to kill her! My inner voice screamed in terror, though I sat there silent and motionless. I allowed myself only to grip the arm of the couch. I wanted to charge him and hit him as hard as I could. This wouldn't be happening if I wasn't so small. Like so many times before, I wanted to grow up, to be big. I wanted to be so big that he would think twice before hitting any of us.

But there was nothing I could do.

Growing tired, he reached down and slowly took her by the hair. He pulled her head up, presenting her to me. Her breathing was raspy, her face beginning to swell with blood streaming down her nose. He studied her for a moment, looking her face up and down as if to determine what to do next.

This was it. He was going to kill her.

"See what happens when you talk back to a man?" he asked as he looked at me in disgust. "Who'm I kiddin'? You're just like her… too stupid to see anything unless it smacks you in the face."

He continued to hold her head up, looking between the two of us. Her eyes were closed now. I wasn't sure if she was still alive or not. It wasn't until she finally spoke that I knew she was still with us.

"I… want. I want a divorce."

He looked at her, the shock sobering him up. He seemed as if he was at a loss for words.

"All right, that's enough." He looked down at my mother as she was dropped back to the floor. "So, you want a divorce, huh?"

He then took her by the hair and began dragging her down the hall. She didn't even have the strength to grab his hands to keep him from pulling her hair out. Her body fell limp as he pulled her toward their bedroom, closing the door behind them.

I looked down at the floor where she had been a few moments prior. The only thing left was blood on the carpet and clumps of black hair.

She had sacrificed herself for me, taking the abuse to keep me from meeting the same fate. It was all my fault. I wasn't sure how he was expecting me to fight those boys since I didn't know how to fight, but it didn't matter. It wasn't fair.

I winced as I felt a tap on my shoulder. Scott was there with my Walkman and headphones.

"Come on. You know the drill. We need to go to our rooms."

He knew this routine well, and since he was older by seven years, he tried to take care of me. "Listen to your music," he whispered, directing me back to the room we shared. That was how my mom dealt with things. She bought me a Walkman so I could drown out the noise when he beat her.

Inside our room, my brother and I sat together on my bed and just waited. He gently put the headphones on my head and rubbed my back. I took them off right away. I needed to make sure mom was still alive.

A short time later, we heard their door open and heavy footsteps lumber down the hall. We peeked out the window as we heard our father open the front door and leave the house. He had two suitcases with him and was proceeding to throw them in the back of our old Lincoln. He was moving smoothly for being so drunk. We watched as he pulled the car out of the driveway and out of sight.

We sat and waited. It was so silent in our room that I could hear my heart thundering in my chest. We were listening for Mom to move, but not a sound came from their room. We looked at each other. Did he kill her? Even Scott looked worried. This differed from the other times our father beat our mother unconscious. She usually made noise by now.

I remember not knowing if we were going to be orphans, or worse yet, being forced to go live with him on our own.

After what seemed an eternity, we finally heard some movement from inside their room, along with some coughing. She was still alive. I wanted to go out to her, but your uncle held me back, reminding me of the rule: never leave the room until she came to get you.

Then I heard the spinning of the rotary phone they kept on their nightstand. I didn't even breathe until I heard her voice.

"It's over," she said. "I told him I wanted a divorce. No, I'm okay."

It was a few minutes into the conversation that we noticed her do something we had never heard before: she was sobbing uncontrollably, going on about how she had pulled the trigger, and now she didn't know what to do. I pressed my ear against the door, taking in everything she was saying.

He was gone, gone to live with the woman he'd been seeing behind her back. She didn't care about the beatings, she said, but finding out that he'd been cheating on her was what hurt the most. It was infidelity that was the final straw for her.

I went back to my twin-size bed and tried to understand what this meant about love. How could anyone hurt someone they loved like that? I hated hearing my mother cry like that. Hearing her like that was like a knife to my gut. That night was my fault, and I was going to make it right. Even back then, somehow, I knew I had the ability to change the future.

You won't be like that; I heard a voice in my head say. *And when you meet your girlfriend, she'll never be like Mom is now. She'll never cry, or get hurt, or anything. You will be loyal to her, no matter what. Your kids will never have to deal with this, either. It's all up to you to change things.*

The thought comforted me. Within a half hour, Grandma Leona, my father's mother, came over. Shortly after, flashing blue and red lights illuminated our driveway. They took my mother to the hospital with three cracked ribs, a broken orbital bone, and multiple lacerations throughout her body. But we survived.

The night was over.

• •

We moved around Florida for the next two years, bouncing from house to house. The divorce went through, and Mom married a man named Dick. She'd met him through her nursing job.

In 1988, we moved into a small house on Fairhaven Street. Another house, another beginning. On our first day there, I noticed some movement across the street as I brought in boxes from the moving van. When I came back outside, it was then that I saw her.

There, standing beside the main road, was the most beautiful girl I had ever seen. The vision before me wore a fuzzy pink bathrobe with a blue flower on its right lapel, a lapel that was lightly blanketed with dark blonde locks. She was chewing on her right index finger as she peeked around the van. Waving over at me, a smile crossed her face as we laid eyes on each other for the very first time. This beautiful little stranger would change the trajectory of our family forever.

3

"Secret Garden"
(by Bruce Springsteen)

Just as quickly as she had appeared, she vanished. My mother conveniently distracted me for a moment with a question just long enough to keep me from seeing where she went. I tried to return my attention back to the mystery girl as quickly as I could, but the spot where she'd stood was now empty. I did not know where she'd come from and no idea where she'd gone.

My focus was gone for the rest of the day. The image of her had embedded in my psyche like a splinter. I couldn't put my finger on it, but I felt something in those moments we made eye contact. It was like Alka-Seltzer in my brain, a tingling that began in my head and spread through my extremities all the way to my nails.

I was both calm and racked with nerves at the same time. Something seemed unique about this girl, special even. The longer I thought about it, the more it drove me crazy. The last thing I needed was yet another girl making fun of me, but something pulled me toward her. I had to see her again.

That night, the image of the mystery girl bounced around in my mind like a renegade pinball. When my first alarm went off in the morning, I was still thinking about her. Then my second alarm went off.

"Christopher! Get your butt up! You're going to be late for your first day of school!"

At least she wasn't calling me C.J. anymore. I looked out my bedroom window, hoping the girl would be there.

Nothing. My heart sank as I got dressed and I dragged myself over to the dining room table. Dick sat at one end, looking up from his newspaper and morning cigarette just long enough to glare at me disapprovingly.

"Took you long enough."

That was his usual greeting in the morning. His ability to sniff out things wrong with me rivaled most bloodhounds. He differed from my father in that he didn't hit us, but the lack of physical violence made way for a razor-sharp tongue. He returned to his newspaper as my mother dutifully sat his morning coffee in front of him.

Then she set down a bowl in front of me. The steam rising from it hit me square in the face. *Not oatmeal, not again.* It was Mom's staple, especially on days when we were in a hurry. With me, she defaulted to quick and easy so she could return her attention to whatever Dick needed.

Somehow, Dick could sense I wasn't eating because his newspaper slowly lowered again. "What's wrong?" he mocked. "Little baby doesn't like his oatmeal? It's bad enough that your mother waits on you hand and foot, just to have you turn your nose up to it. EAT."

I met his glare with one of my own and stabbed the bowl with my spoon.

"Christopher!" Mom yelled from the kitchen. "You break my bowl; I'm going to be pissed!"

One day I'll be on my own and I'll never eat oatmeal again. Thirty years later, I'm still eating oatmeal, thanks to your mom.

I downed my bland breakfast and finished getting ready. Mom was impatiently standing at the front door with my backpack. She kissed me on the head after I donned my gear and sent me out for my first day at my new school.

I set off on the quarter-mile trek to the bus stop, where Fairhaven intersected with Crocus. As I got nearer, I noticed a couple of kids already standing there. They were difficult to make out at first but took the shape of two girls as I approached. Both were wearing their own backpacks, and it appeared as if they were arguing.

One had curly platinum blonde hair and was tall and skinny. She was the more animated of the two, waving her arms back and forth while yelling at the other. As the moments passed, the conversation appeared to sour, for she was now stomping the ground in protest, her arms rigid at her sides with clenched fists.

The other's hair was darker, a dirty blonde. She held the straps to her backpack and argued back with the blonde, though she seemed fed up with the conversation.

Noticing me now, the lighter blonde ceased her tirade and stared. When I was close enough to engage in conversation, she waved. I shyly returned the gesture.

"Is this the bus stop for Fairhaven?" I asked, my voice low.

"Yes!" the younger one answered. "I'm Michelle!"

"I'm Chris," I said politely. It was at that point that the darker blonde turned to look at me.

It was her. The girl from yesterday, this time in a blue T-shirt and gray shorts. I stopped dead in my tracks as the realization set in. She gave the same captivating smile as before.

"I'm Danielle," she said, reaching her hand out. It was when I reached out to shake her hand that I noticed her eyes. She had the most stunning emerald eyes that shimmered when she smiled. A smattering of freckles lay under each eye, her cheeks pink below them.

My brain commanded my tongue to move, but it refused. "Hi!" she said excitedly. "You're the new guy across the street from us! I saw you yesterday."

I blushed.

"Were you spying, Danielle?" Michelle chimed in. Danielle launched a sideways look at her, but that didn't deter her from continuing. "I'm gonna tell Mom and Dad! You know you're not supposed to go to a stranger's house without our parents meeting them first!"

So they're sisters!

"Shut up, Michelle," Danielle launched back. "Why don't you go look for the bus? It's your turn."

"I don't want to!" Michelle cried.

"Look, I'm the oldest here. You do as I say!"

The two locked eyes. Neither was going to back down. I tried to ignore the awkwardness of the situation by looking around.

Michelle finally growled in frustration and slammed her backpack on the ground. She turned and marched down Crocus toward the curve, screaming the entire way down. "SO UNFAIR! I WANT TO STAY AND MEET CHRIS TOO!"

Danielle let out a lingering sigh as she watched her sister shrink into the distance. I stared at the two of them as if they had two heads apiece. Both wanted to hang out with me? What kind of story twist was this?

"Sorry," she sighed dramatically. "Sisters... this is how we are! Do you have any sisters or brothers?"

"I have an older brother. He's seven years older than I am."

"Wow!" she remarked. "That's a big difference! I'm only three years older than Michelle. Does he yell at you and beat you up?"

I looked down at the ground.

"He can be annoying."

She laughed. I couldn't tell if she was laughing at me or not. The confusion made me uneasy. I was still waiting for the other shoe to drop, for her to turn on me and begin making fun of me. She seemed genuine and kind, but then again, so did lots of people who hurt me.

We talked for another ten minutes as Michelle waited at the far end of the street by the turn barrier. Danielle was chattier than any girl I had ever met. She talked a lot about her family: what her parents did for work, where they liked to go on summer vacation, even how she and Michelle would sleep in the same bed when they stayed at their grandparents' house. It seemed like they all really liked each other.

In between stories about her life, she sprinkled in questions about my family: where we came from, what my parents did for a living. I said very little, omitting where I had come from.

The more we talked, the closer she stood to me. The closer she stood to me, the more tingling I felt in my body. I was a bundle of nerves when she stood right next to me as she spoke. I had never been that close to a girl before. It seemed second nature to her.

She stopped talking for a moment as she looked down at Michelle's backpack, which lay on the side of the road.

"Watch this!" she grinned. With a single movement of her arm, she snatched the blue backpack and quickly flung it into the grassy field next to us. It landed in a muddy puddle nearby. Danielle giggled excitedly, proud of her handiwork.

I looked at this beautiful girl in disbelief.

That was mean. I gripped harder onto the straps of my backpack.

She looked back at me and put her hands on her hips. Somehow, she could see my disappointment.

"Hey," she said, "sisters, remember? She's done worse to me!"

I nodded but didn't really believe her. How could someone so breathtaking be so mean?

I pushed the event out of my mind as Michelle suddenly came running toward us as fast as she could. "BUS! BUS!"

Rounding the curb behind her came the large yellow school bus. As hard as she tried to outrun it, it sped past her and pulled up next to us. Danielle looked on as Michelle panted and heaved onward. "Michelle! Get your backpack!" she yelled at her sister. Then, turning to me, she said, "Come on. You're with me."

• •

We arrived at school and parted ways. Danielle was in fourth grade, a grade higher than me, so she had a different class. She smiled as she walked away, almost running into another student as she went along. She apologized and waved one last time as she left my sight.

Although it was my first day of school, all I could do was watch the clock. I couldn't wait until 3:30 when I could find her again. For the first time in my life, I liked a girl.

Finally, the bell rang, and we met on the bus. Danielle sat next to me, and we lowered our heads in the seat so no one else could hear us. She regaled me with the events of her day: lunch was bland, but she really liked history because they learned about France. She told me how she wanted to go to Paris one day.

Before long, we were walking home with Michelle running ahead in a huff. We continued to talk the entire time, and I felt my walls slowly coming down. We stopped in front of my house. She swayed shyly as we struggled to find something else to say instead of goodbye.

That was one of the most magical moments in my life, perhaps my first magical moment. Despite our awkwardness, I like to think that was when we both recognized the special connection we would share for the rest of our lives. But eventually, the awkwardness was more than I could handle.

"I'll see you tomorrow," I said.

"Hey," she said, stopping me, "I hope I get to see you real soon!" Now it was her turn to blush. "I mean, since we're neighbors and all. Come over anytime you want! No pressure."

I smiled as she turned to walk away. I watched as she approached her door, waving one final time before disappearing inside.

I floated the rest of the way to my house. I'd never felt that good ever in my life. It was as if everything that had ever happened to me before melted away. It was the beginning of my journey to become the man I was destined to be, the journey that would ultimately give me the greatest gift I have ever had: the two of you and your mother.

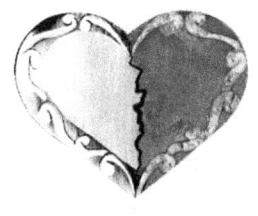

4

"Uptown Girl"
(by Billy Joel)

The last thing I ever expected was to fall in love. But life turns on a dime sometimes, and by the end of summer, my friendship with Danielle had transformed me. And within a year and a half, this girl would become my girlfriend, conferring upon me a status I'd never dreamed possible for myself.

But it took a great deal to get to that point. It started with taking Danielle up on her invitation to visit and meet her family. Her parents were not exactly welcoming, but they tolerated their daughter's new companion, or, as her mom put it, her "little friend."

Her father accepted my presence but did not approve of who I was as a person. As time went on, I spent more and more time there, which exposed him to my less-desirable traits. I frustrated him with my tendency to give up when things got difficult. That, with my looks and physical weakness, made for a boy who wasn't good enough for his daughter, or so I overheard one day when they were in the kitchen.

"I don't know what she sees in that kid."

"What's the big deal?" her mom said, putting away the dishes. The clanging made me have to strain to hear them. "They're only friends, hon."

"Only friends?" he scoffed. "That's how it starts. You and I were only friends in the beginning, remember?"

My heart sank when I overheard them. I just wanted to be accepted, given a chance, maybe even a little encouragement. I was only ten years old.

"Just go with it, okay?" her mom finished. "Danielle has been wanting a friend since we moved here. We want her to be happy."

But Danielle was getting frustrated with me, too. I was closed off, and she pushed me to come out of my shell. She would have me take Polaroid pictures of her posing like a supermodel. Danielle always was and still is a natural ham.

"Come on!" she'd call to me, grabbing the camera. "Your turn! Pose for me!"

I just stood there, my shoulders rolled forward, my hands tucked deep in the pockets of my blue jeans.

"Chris! Come on!" she pleaded.

I shrugged apologetically. It was difficult for her to understand that I wasn't an outgoing person. Still, she was determined.

She realized in time that the best way to open me up was through conversation. We talked about everything, our hopes and our dreams. Beneath a poster of the Eiffel Tower, beside another of New Kids on the Block, she gushed about her dream to go to Paris. She wanted to see it from the very top of the tower at night.

We also spent a lot of time together without talking much. We would crash on the couch and watch *Chip and Dale's Rescue Rangers*. Her dad would closely monitor us, especially when we were in her room alone. He'd suddenly barge in and demand that she keep the door open.

"Dad! We're not doing anything wrong!"

"I don't care! He's still a boy. Those are the rules!"

Eventually, I began sharing details of my past about school and what I went through. I realized I trusted her. She was the first person I ever truly and completely opened myself up to.

"And you thought I was going to mistreat you, like the other girls?" she asked as we sat on the couch. I nodded. "I would never do that to you!" She seemed offended that I'd even had the thought. "Now everything about you makes sense."

I smiled as she touched my arm gently. It felt amazing to share those painful details of my past without judgment. I could finally understand the phrase, "a weight lifted off my shoulders."

I drew in a deep breath. "That's not all," I continued. I felt like I needed to tell her everything. She seemed like she would be okay with it. It was an enormous risk, but with her, I felt brave enough to talk about it. "It wasn't just the kids at school who did that stuff to me."

I told her about my father, how he hit us, how he almost killed my mother the day he moved out, and how they eventually divorced. I told her how my family talked to me, how they expected me to turn out just like my father, who they had said was just like his father. Danielle's face slowly shifted from just listening to deep sadness.

I looked over and spotted her mom in the doorway. She was also tearing up. Her father had joined her and was listening as well. His normal grumpy demeanor was melting before my eyes.

When I ran out of things to say, I looked down at my feet in shame. *Maybe I just screwed everything up, like always. No way will Danielle want to hang out with me now. No way will her parents let me keep coming around.*

But she sprung forward and wrapped her arms around me. She buried her face in my shoulder and cried. It was the first time someone other than my mother or grandmother had ever hugged me.

Her parents stayed in the doorway and communicated with each other through a look. Her mom then looked back over at me. "Is that where you go every other weekend, to your father's?"

I nodded.

"Does he still hit you?"

I said nothing. Her dad cleared his throat uncomfortably. Danielle held me tight as I put my head down on her shoulder.

"You're uh... you're welcome here any time," he said matter-of-factly.

And they meant it. Their house became my sanctuary. When Mom and Dick fought, I went to Danielle's house. From that point forward, I felt like a part of their family. Wherever I was, Danielle was there. And wherever she was, so was I. She brought out a side of my personality that was warm and caring, and the two of us became best friends.

My world seemed brighter with her and her family. There was no fighting, no hitting, no insults. They had a deep love and appreciation for each other. They seemed to actually like each other, to enjoy being a family, and now I was part of that.

I don't recall a happier time ever in my life than when I was with them.

• •

That all changed one hot summer's eve. The day was like any other, Danielle and I hanging out and listening to music, sharing my headphones. Her dad had relaxed his "door open" rule, provided we agreed to behave, which we always did, so we could finally enjoy some privacy.

That day, Danielle disappeared for a short while after Michelle had called for her. I laid on her bed, continuing to listen to my music. It wasn't until I saw Daniele storm back in and slam the door shut I realized something was amiss. She growled in fury as I took the headphones off.

"What's wrong?"

"I can't *believe* her…" she seethed, storming back and forth.

I looked at her, confused.

"What are you talking about, Danielle?"

Suddenly, I heard Michelle bang on her door.

"Open the door, Danielle! What's the big deal? It's just a bet! You scared you're gonna lose?"

Danielle's face was a bright crimson red. With a sudden twist, she yanked the door open. Michelle stood at the entrance with one boy from the neighborhood. Danielle came within an inch of her sister's face.

"I will not do it!"

Michelle looked in at me and raised her eyebrows. "You got anyone else?" she asked her sister.

Danielle pouted angrily and shook her head no.

"What is going on?" I asked poignantly. I had a feeling it had something to do with me.

"I challenged Danielle to a contest," Michelle began. "The loser does the winner's chores for a week!"

I waited for the point.

"It's a kissing contest," Danielle said, exasperated. "Each of us must kiss a boy for as long as we can. The longest kiss wins."

"And since Danielle doesn't have a boyfriend like I do, that leaves you as her only choice for a partner."

Danielle's eyes were lit with fury. Trevor, Michelle's new boyfriend, had been an area of friction between the two sisters because Michelle bragged about him incessantly. The fact that she was the first to get a boyfriend elated her to no end. At one point, I thought it was going to turn into a fistfight between them. But then I remembered this family wasn't like that.

"Oh," I said nervously. "Do you wanna do it?"

"No!"

"Why not?" Michelle demanded. "Because of how he looks?"

Danielle was fuming in anger. She'd become very protective of me, especially at school. She was ready to throw down with anyone who besmirched me.

"It's fine, Danielle. I get it. You don't have to do it," I tried to reassure her before the fur flew between the two of them. She looked at me and her eyes were watering. "I get it," I repeated. "I'm ugly. It's okay. We don't have to kiss. I'm happy we're friends."

"First, you're not ugly," Danielle said, wiping a tear from her eye. "And second, that's not the point! That's not something friends do!"

I gave her a half smile as she put her hands on her hips and sighed again.

"Okay, so you lose by forfeit!" Michelle yelled. "You do my chores for a week!" Then she ran out of the room.

"That's not fair!" Danielle screamed and bolted out the door after her.

A minute later, I went to see where they went and found the three of them beside the house near the tire swing.

"Oh good, he's here," Michelle said. "Let the contest begin!" I slid up to Danielle and said nothing. "This is going to be easy," Michelle happily cried out. "Now count!" Their lips met, and Danielle counted begrudgingly to seventeen.

"Your turn," Michelle laughed, tearing her face away from Trevor's. Danielle's face dropped. This was getting very real.

Danielle paced in front of me, conflicted and overwhelmed. I hated seeing her like that, but I didn't know what to do. And, I admit, my feelings were getting hurt, too. I felt humiliated. Until this point, I had almost forgotten about my unfortunate looks because I was so happy just being accepted. My stomach twisted and turned inside me as flashbacks to my past haunted me.

Collecting herself, Danielle took a deep breath and looked me in the eye.

"Really, it's fine. We don't have to—"

"NO!" she yelled, waving her hand. "I'm doing this!" She stepped forward, moving her face within inches of mine.

Michelle egged her on, saying, "You don't have the guts!"

But then Danielle grabbed my shoulders and pulled me in, pressing her lips against mine.

Boys, let me tell you, there is nothing like that proper first kiss.

It started out forced, our lips mashed together with Danielle holding me tight to make sure we didn't separate. We seemed to melt together as Michelle's count became muffled in the background. Just before my own eyes closed, I saw Danielle's eyebrows go up a little before she closed hers.

I could feel electricity surging and crackling between the two of us. The hair on my arms stood on end as goosebumps emerged and spread up to my elbows. My legs quivered like jelly as we sank further into the experience. My heartbeat thundered in my head and had to of been going a mile a minute. For a short time, we were joined in the most exquisite sense of confusion and excitement rolled into one, and I didn't want it to end.

"All right!" Michelle barked. "Stop! Ew! God, gross!"

Danielle blinked in disbelief as we slowly came apart. She put her hand over her chest as she tried to catch her breath. A smile warily crossed her face as her eyes widened.

She looked at me as if seeing me for the first time. A small giggle emerged as she pulled our foreheads together. We looked into each other's eyes and, for the first time, saw something more than friendship.

Then she sang. "You lose, lose, lose!" She quickly gave me one last peck on the lips, grabbed me by the hand, and started running us back to the house.

"I'm gonna tell Dad he's your boyfriend!" Michelle called after us. "He's gonna be so mad!"

Danielle smiled at me as she turned the knob to the door.

"I'm okay with that," she grinned.

5

"Just the Way You Are"
(by Billy Joel)

"You're not in love with her," my mother scolded. "You're only eleven!"

That's how it was with my mom. She always insisted that she knew better than me what I thought and felt and whether it was justified.

Her brown eyes stared at me icily, her right hand pressing the phone to her chest.

I had made two mistakes: one; I had interrupted an important phone call she was on, and two, I shared my feelings with her, which was something I had learned not too long ago.

My mother was a "glass half-empty" kind of person, parading around as a realist. Her philosophy of life centered on worst-case scenario anticipation. For her, the worst case was the norm. Unfortunately, scenarios also included people, and no one was immune.

She blamed my father, of course. She wouldn't be so distrustful of everyone and everything if the man who told her he loved her didn't treat her so badly. In her mind, everyone was out to get her. Everyone was an incompetent idiot who was one stupid decision away from ruining her life or their own.

On the battlefield that was her world, she kept her rifle affixed to her cheek, anxiously awaiting the enemy she knew was coming from the fog of life. Her itchy trigger finger was a byproduct of her belief that everyone was going to hurt her. She couldn't wait for someone to prove her pessimism right so she could justify pulling the trigger.

When I say no one was immune, that also included me. I was helpless against her worst-case scenario-assumptions about everything I thought and believed. It didn't matter to her what I'd been through or how quickly I'd had to grow up because of it. I was still just a dumb kid, wet behind the ears and clueless, and, according to my mother, destined to become just like my father.

I had stormed into our house just minutes before, on the verge of tears. Seeing my mother on the way in, I submitted to an uncontrollable urge to tell her exactly what had happened: the girl I loved had broken my heart.

"You don't love her," she said.

"Yes, I do!" I screamed back, red in the face. "You know nothing!"

The look she gave me then told me I'd gone too far. "Let me call you back," she said after returning the receiver to her ear. "I gotta take care of something."

I was expecting the worst as she'd taught me to do, but she just took a deep breath.

"Alright. What happened?"

"Danielle started hanging out with these other guys," I said, my voice breaking, "and now it's like I don't even exist!"

My mother studied me for a moment. I couldn't tell if she was feeling sorry for me or not. The hesitancy she displayed was very uncharacteristic. She was always quick to dole out punishment if I dared raise my voice to her.

"I never liked her, and you know it," she said, shrugging her shoulders. "It doesn't surprise me she hurt you. What have I told you before? All it takes is one poor decision and your life is ruined. Your father taught me that. Love will only hurt you. Better you learn that lesson sooner than later."

I looked up at her. All I wanted was some sympathy, some reassurance that everything would be okay. Instead, she gave me the same blank, unemotional look she got every time anything got too real.

"And your heart's not broken," she continued. "You're too young to know what you're talking about. Did you tell her you love her?"

I shook my head no.

"Has she told you she loves you?"

Again, no.

"See? I'm right. You're better off, anyway. Nothing good can come of it."

With that, the conversation was over. I sulked away to the front door with my head low. Outside, I sat on the front step and looked over at Danielle's house. I could hear an occasional giggle or playful scream through its open windows. The longer I watched, the more I could feel my blood come to boil. What were they doing in there?

After everything we'd been through, she replaced me. *I finally get to have someone amazing in my life, just to have them snatched away by a group of punks who think they're better than me?*

All four of the new guys were bigger than I was. All four were better looking as well. They rode by on their bikes when we were outside and Danielle, being Danielle, welcomed them to join us.

Within two hours, they'd infiltrated their way in and told me to get lost. She didn't object. Instead, when I tried to tell her I didn't like these guys, she raised her voice in frustration and said, "Then leave!"

This wasn't our first fight.

After the kiss, everything really had changed, not just between us, but within me. Since I was essentially part of the family, I was being teased and yelled at like one of them. It wasn't long before I started dishing it out, too, finally secure enough to give voice to my opinions.

"Go home and don't come back!" she would scream after I got on her last nerve. I'd storm off, and we'd give each other the silent treatment for a few hours or a day before one of us would show up to apologize.

But as I looked across the street now, I had a terrifying new thought: *What if we don't make up this time?* I looked back into my house and saw my mother sitting with Dick at the dining table.

She'd love that if I lost my only friend. She would get to be right. It's all she cares about. She doesn't care that they ripped my heart out. "It's your own fault," she says. One poor decision!

I was done with girls. She was just like all the others. Or so I thought. My head shot up as I heard her scream across the street.

"Don't you ever!" She sounded mad.

Michelle probably said something.

"Get out!"

There goes Michelle.

"Get out of my house!!"

Her house?

Then she screamed like I'd never heard her scream before. There was nothing playful about it. It was a call of warning, or of danger.

My body jumped up before my brain knew what was happening.

If any of them hurt her...

I pounded on their door with my fist, but when no one came, I just barged in.

All four guys came stampeding from her room, with Danielle right behind them. They all gave me dirty looks as they passed.

"You're never welcome back here again!" she screamed as they bounded out the door and onto their bikes.

"But he's such a loser!" one of them yelled back.

"He's my boyfriend! Now get out of here before I call my dad!" She growled under her breath in frustration as she watched them ride down Fairhaven. Michelle came out and held up her hands as if to say, *What gives?*

Danielle waved her off. "I don't want to talk about it," she grumbled, storming past us both back into the house, slamming the door behind her.

I followed Michelle up toward Danielle's room. Michelle knocked on the door. "Go away!" Danielle yelled. Michelle gave a shrug and left. I tried knocking on the door myself.

"I SAID GO AWAY, MICHELLE!"

"It's me," I whispered. There was silence for a moment as I waited to hear my fate.

"You can come in," she said, her voice lowering. I cautiously opened the door and entered. She sat atop the edge of her bed, doubled over, her face in her hands.

I sat next to her. The two of us just sat still in the moment. She cleared her throat a few times. I could tell she had been crying, though she was trying desperately to hide it.

"They left in a hurry," I said, trying to break the awkward silence.

"Yep," she said bluntly, wiping away a tear. "Serves them right, too."

It wasn't the first time she had jumped on people for what they said about me in her presence. She had always brushed off the act of defending me as if it wasn't a big deal. This one hit her hard.

"So, what happened?" I asked.

"They were talking about you. I told them to leave. That's all."

"What did they say that made you so upset?" I asked, wanting more information.

"I'm not repeating it," she said. "It was bad. It doesn't matter, anyway. They aren't welcome back here. Ever." She continued to wipe her eyes with her hands, then looked at them and groaned in frustration. She hated crying in front of people.

"You didn't have to do that," I told her, wanting to make her feel better. "You don't have to banish them if they're your friends."

I'll never forget the look she gave me, as if I'd just said something that disgusted her. My face flushed in shame.

She's going to get pissed at me now.

But instead of anger, there was a tone of disappointment in her voice. "You mean way more to me than you know," she said. "I'm not going to just stand by and listen while someone talks in front of me about someone I love. You deserve better than that. They're lucky I didn't hit them!"

Love? Did she just say love? Everything else dissolved, the guys, the tears, all the other words. *Did she just tell me she loves me?*

Noticing the look on my face, she chuckled.

"You just now figured that out?" she said, acting like it was no big deal. I could only stare at her in disbelief. I'd already considered myself lucky just to have a friend, then to have a girlfriend, but now someone who loved me. Here in front of me was the most beautiful girl I had ever seen, and she *loved me. ME, of all people.* She just said it.

"You love me?"

She rolled her eyes. "Yes, Chris. I love you. Is that really that surprising? We're together, like, all the time."

"Actually..." I said, looking down at my feet. I felt another wave of shame come over me.

"Hey," she softly whispered, motioning for me to look at her, "why don't you feel you deserve to be loved?"

"I don't know." It was all I could muster as a response. "I guess I still have a hard time believing that someone like you would like me, let alone love me."

Danielle's mood shifted back to frustration. My stubborn adherence to this self-defeating attitude about myself had finally pushed her too far. Most girls would give up on a guy by this point, but Danielle was loyal. Composing herself with a deep breath, she waited a moment before speaking.

"I never cared about how you look, you know. You're a great guy, and I'm happy you're in my life."

I just stared at her, lost in her green eyes and her beautiful face. Now I was the one welling up with tears. She was a veritable angel, the answer to my prayers.

God exists.

Sure, she was an angel with a temper, but it was because she was a passionate person. We were both passionate. I saw that now. Inside that shy shell she kept helping me crack, I also had passion. At this point in my life, it was all for her.

"Besides," she continued, nudging me with her elbow, "no one teases you but me."

We both laughed. She looked up at the Eiffel Tower on her wall, trying to regain her composure. I looked only at her, trying to understand what this meant for me.

At that moment, I remembered my mother on the phone before she went to the hospital. *I will never let Danielle feel anything close to that.* And then I had an epiphany.

Danielle was *the* girl. She was the one I'd marry, the girl I would love so much, and so truly that no one could ever say I was anything like my father. I would prove my mother wrong and break the family cycle of beaten sons turning into abusive men. Being loved by Danielle made it all seem easy. More than easy. It was my destiny.

Even at eleven years old, I knew it in my gut.

Danielle got up and went over to her white vanity to clean herself up. I watched, transfixed, as she wiped her face and ran a brush through her hair. In her mirror's reflection, I didn't see the girl next door. I saw my wife getting ready for us to go out for a night on the town. I heard the babysitter reading to our kids in the next room. She opened a drawer and pulled out a sparkly tube of strawberry lip gloss. She smacked her lips together after rubbing it on with her finger.

"You know," she said, still fixed on her own reflection, "my dad always says other people are the mirrors for what we think of ourselves. If we don't think we deserve something, we can't expect anyone else to disagree. You need to change the way you think, Chris. You deserve to be happy, duh! But until you believe it yourself..."

She stopped when she noticed my eyes locked on her.

"What?" she said with a confused smile.

I love you; I thought. *She said it, why can't I say it? Just say it. I love you!* But I could only smile back at her.

She rolled her eyes and returned to the mirror.

She loved me. There was no longer any room for doubt about it. She loved me, not because she took pity on me, or because she was obligated to, but because I was a person deserving of love. Not a freak, not stupid, not perfect either, but a person who deserved happiness. I decided once and for all that I would change my mindset from that point forward. She deserved a brave and confident man. I deserved to be happy, and she deserved a man who believed that about himself. It was that mindset that helped me endure the seven and a half years of hell that were just around the corner.

I reached over and put my arm around her, pulling her into me from the side. She leaned in, closed her eyes, and sighed happily.

"You're such a weirdo," she giggled.

I turned and kissed her on the side of the head, as she had done to me so many times before in the past.

"I love you, too," I whispered in her ear.

For an instant, the entire world came to a halt. It was as if our lives had led to that moment, where it was only the two of us. But the world would start spinning again soon, and fast.

As my girlfriend became more than ever-present in my life, she became more at risk of encountering the demons of my past. Despite my efforts to shield Danielle, she was about to come face-to-face with my father, and as I would soon find out, there was little I could do to protect her when things spiraled out of control.

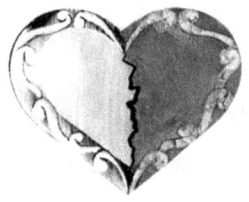

6

"Dance of the Prince and the Sugar-Plum Fairy"
(by Pyotr Ilyich Tchaikovsky)

I should have known something bad was going to happen. I found my gut twisting more than it usually did. It always twisted when it knew something was about to happen. It was trying to tell me that Danielle was in danger in our house, to get her out of there because something terrible was about to happen.

Warning signs were popping up everywhere. My mother was more on edge, especially when Danielle was around. When I told her that Danielle and I said "I love you" to each other, she immediately dismissed it. She and Dick were fighting more often about anything and everything, though my behavior was a popular topic. She also took more phone calls from my father, which always ended in a screaming match. Twice we overheard her tell Dick that my father was threatening to come over "and deal with this face-to-face."

"Good! Let him! I got something for him!" Dick would bark.

Of all the fears I had at twelve, the biggest by far was that my father would get his hands on Danielle. They were two of the most bullheaded people I knew. If they met, anything could happen.

Her willingness to stand up to anyone was one of the many things I loved about her. But it bordered on eagerness. But my father was a grown man, with a violent and criminal past, and she was four foot ten and eighty-seven pounds.

I would see Danielle in my mother's place in my nightmares, crumbling under the blow of my father's gnarly hands. It chilled me to the bone and kept me up. Would he hit a little girl, someone he outweighed by more than one hundred pounds? I imagined he could. Most frightening of all, I would be powerless to stop it. I knew the longer she stayed with us, the more likely she was to encounter him.

That day came in the spring of 1990. I met Danielle over at her house after eating Sunday breakfast at home. We hung out in her room for a bit until her mom called up for Danielle to do her chores. She groaned and took her time getting up.

"Chris, you can watch TV down here if you'd like to wait. I'm tempted to have you help since you're here so much, though."

"I'm okay with that!" she quickly retorted, glancing at me with a sly smile. Her mom stood before her, hands on hips in anticipation of her daughter dragging her feet.

Danielle reluctantly did as they instructed her while I sat on the couch. Danielle stuck her tongue out while I teased her by sprawling out and pretending to sleep. I laughed and winced as she snuck over and playfully smacked me on the stomach. Luckily, that smack was enough for forgiveness as we were making faces at each other by the time she finished. We retreated to the side of the house afterward to swing on the tire swing.

"Don't push me high," she demanded with a smile. "I don't want to fall like I did last time!"

"Whatever… I caught you!" I argued.

"Seriously?" she remarked as she slid into the swing.

Naturally, I pushed it as high as I could. Danielle let out a screech as the tire shot into the air. Each push made her scream a little louder.

I grinned as she swung by me, proud of my work. Each time she passed, I would pretend to reach out to grab the line, only to give the tire another push.

"STOP THE TIRE! STOP THE TIRE!" she screamed between laughs. It was difficult to tell if she was giggling more than screaming. Choosing to err on the side of caution, I reached out and grabbed the rope to stop it.

"You jerk! You know I hate that!" she yelled, trying to pout but unable to hide a grin. As soon as she released her death grip on the tire, she reached over and punched me in the arm.

"I'm sorry," I said, sarcasm dripping from my voice. She fumed again and jumped back on the swing.

"Push me again, but nice this time!"

I was reaching for the swing when I noticed some movement coming from my driveway across the street. She looked back to see why I wasn't doing as I was told, turning her attention to what had stolen mine.

There were three people outside my house. I couldn't hear what they were saying, but from the looks of their animated body language, two of them were arguing with the third. Danielle got off and joined me as I cautiously walked over to the end of her driveway.

Mom and Dick were arguing with the bigger, angrier person in front of them. That person was my father.

I came to a stop right at the sidewalk when I realized it was him. He was yelling and gesticulating in a wild rage. He had lived up to his threat of coming over. "This is bullshit! You will not get away with this!"

"It's happening, whether you like it or not!" she screamed back.

"You bitch! I have rights!"

"We'll let the court decide that."

"You fucking—" he howled in anger. My eyes widened as I watched him lunge forward to hit her, but Dick stepped in and stopped him. Then all hell broke loose.

I froze in fear. I watched the situation escalate, my feet unable to move. Flashbacks to my previous life flooded my head. In those moments, I was six years old again.

But this time was different. This time, the grasp of a small hand interrupted my fear, its fingers intertwining with mine. The grip was gentle, but strong enough to tell me I wasn't alone.

There was Danielle, right by my side. Her jaw was clenched as she shifted slightly behind me. I had never seen her so tense before. Amid the chaos unfolding in front of us, I could see just how scared she was. I found myself more concerned about her than about the fight happening in front of us.

My father was screaming and cursing as they went on, saying that he would kill both of them. Within moments, he had backed off slightly, saying he didn't want to go to prison for the rest of his life. I watched them harangue each other for about twenty seconds before I realized my father had turned his head and noticed the two of us. I could see him perk up at the sight of her, as if he liked what he saw.

"Hey, C.J.," he called over in an unfamiliar voice. "Is that your little girlfriend? Hang on, I'll come over. I want to meet her."

I could hear Danielle breathe out through her nose. She clutched at my left shoulder as he approached. She wanted nothing to do with him. I could tell that one part of her wanted to run up and scream at him, maybe even hit him, but the realization that the stories about him were very real held her back.

My feet thawed. The idea that he might soon be close to her seemed to wake me up. He was getting close, but there was no way I could let him get to her. If she pissed him off, he could seriously hurt her.

His advance was halted instantly by a booming voice nearby.

"Danielle! Get inside right now!"

Her dad came out of the house to see what all the yelling was all about. He walked up and stood in front of us, staring my father down. Danielle's mountain of a father was not backing down.

Danielle slowly backed away but kept her eyes on me while she progressed. I watched her scuttle back toward her house, reluctant to leave me behind.

As she walked away, her dad stepped toward my father, challenging him. I felt relief, not just for his protection but also because I was sure he finally knew what I was dealing with. I was no longer the boy without a backbone. The boy who had become a fixture in his home was just someone with a horrible home life who deserved to be protected.

My father heeded his glare and remained still. After a second, her dad turned and put his arm around me. "Come on, son. Let's go inside," he said. I looked up at him. With a look of understanding, he nodded toward the house.

Like his own child a moment earlier, I did as he said. The two of us proceeded to their front door. He kept his eye on my father the entire time. It was the first time I felt what a father's protection should feel like, the way I try to make you boys feel anytime something goes wrong. But at that moment, I also felt trapped between two clashing families. One family was my past, the other I felt was my future. One family I wanted desperately to leave behind, the other I wanted desperately to join. But only one of them had legal claim to me.

My father stormed over to his truck and drove off, his tires screaming as he launched down Fairhaven. I remember looking up at her dad as we entered the house. He was completely in control. He had stopped my father by simply looking at him. His size and presence were enough to make the intruder turn tail. This was the man I wanted to become: the Protector.

After that, Danielle didn't ask me any more questions about my dad. She had a brief glimpse into how my life had been before Fairhaven Street, and that was enough for her.

The rest of the day was awkward. An enormous shadow seemed to loom over us as the sun set. Her dad was looking at me differently, almost like he felt sorry for me. It was a double-edged sword. While I was glad to have his sympathy finally, it was a reminder that I was still just a child, too weak to have protected his daughter without him. I went about the day with them, too ashamed to say much of anything.

• •

After dinner, Danielle seemed to perk up a bit. To cheer me up, she suddenly grabbed me by the arm and took me into the garage. It was musky from the humidity outside. The concrete floor was covered with old rolled-up carpets, leftovers from her dad's work as a carpenter.

She led me over to two carpets that were stacked longways, side by side, and motioned for me to lie down. I could tell she wanted to cuddle, as we often did, though a damp garage and old stained carpets weren't the usual setting.

We lay next to each other, staring at the ceiling. We reflected on everything that had happened that day.

"Why did your dad call you C.J.?" she asked.

My stomach turned. I'd hoped that name would have stayed out of this part of my life, but somehow it still followed me like a shadow.

"It's a name he calls me. Short for Christopher James."

Looking up at the ceiling, she appeared to be lost in thought. A smile flashed across her face. "I like that name…'C.J.'"

For a moment I thought of objecting, but seeing her smile like that, I couldn't. That smile was the first step I took toward peace with this name and all that it would come to represent to me. Thirty years later, I even capitulated to your mother's request to name one of you C.J. I'm referring to you, Collin James.

Danielle turned onto her side to face me. "Propose to me," she said.

"Huh?"

"Propose to me. Like, show me how you would do it."

"But I don't have a ring," I said, still confused.

She reached into her front pocket and pulled out a gold ring. It had a diamond at the top, with a smaller diamond on both sides. Her mom had yelled at Danielle before for playing with it. This was Danielle's grandmother's engagement ring, a family heirloom. Seeing it now made me feel very nervous because I knew her mom would kill us.

She stuck the ring in my hand and then covered herself with a nearby blanket. She closed her eyes and pretended to go to sleep. Of all the places she wanted a proposal at… while laying on nasty, rolled-up carpets?

I looked at her in disbelief. With my failure to protect her before, she still wanted to marry me? Pretend or not, what kind of husband can't protect his wife? I had hoped as I got older that I could step up when the time came, but I wasn't there yet. I had failed to protect her. When I should have acted, I froze.

Lost in my own thoughts and self-doubt, I heard Danielle clear her throat in annoyance, pushing me to get a move on with it. She was already wife material. I looked at the ring and then back at her.

All I had to do was speak from the heart. After being so exposed earlier, and still loved now, that heart was wide open. I reached over and gently shook her. She opened her eyes and yawned a big, theatrical yawn, stretching her arms over her head, then settling on her side and smiling at me.

"Danielle, I love you more than I could ever say," I began. "I never told you this before, but the day my dad left, I said a prayer to God, asking for someone who would love and accept me…"

She watched me intently. She was no longer pretending.

"God answered that prayer the day we moved to this street. You are my gift from God. He brought you into my life, even though I don't deserve you."

Danielle clicked her tongue and grabbed my hand. "But you do!"

"No, I don't," I interrupted. "I should have protected you today. But I couldn't. I wasn't big enough. Your dad had to step in for me to keep you safe. You deserve a man who can protect you no matter what. I'm not that person right now."

Her eyes watered.

"But because of you, for the first time in my life, I know I can change. Danielle, I am not the man I could be… yet. But if you're willing to be my wife, I promise I will become the man you deserve. I will never fail you again. I will grow up big and strong. I will take care of you and protect you as my wife. I will never hurt you or make you cry. I will be true to you no matter what if you give me the chance."

I could hardly believe how easily this proposal came out of my mouth. I took a deep breath, almost forgetting the most important part:

"Will you be my wife?"

With a sudden blubber, she let out a cry.

"Is that a yes?"

"Yes!" she said. "Yes! Yes! Yes!" I put the ring on what I proudly knew was the correct finger, the ring finger of her left hand. She kissed me and pulled me in for the tightest hug. She continued to sob in my ear as we lay back down under the fluorescent light of the garage. I didn't think she expected that kind of proposal.

We laid together on the nasty, musty carpets. She snuggled against me, her head on my shoulder, listening to my heartbeat. I was so happy

I was glowing. It may have been make believe, but in my mind it was completely real. I believe that was the time the thirty-five-year promise that became this book entered my heart.

My insecurities melted away into the concrete floor of the garage. If she could believe in me, so could I. All that was left was for me to live up to that promise.

Your father is a man of his word.

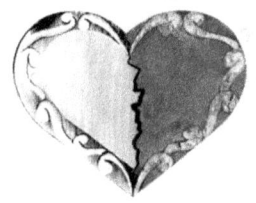

7

"Not While I'm Around"
(from *Sweeney Todd*)

"Chris, please talk to me!" Danielle pleaded as we rode our bikes down Fairhaven Street toward home. I remained silent, pedaling as fast as I could. She stayed along my side, swerving back and forth as she struggled to match my speed.

But I wasn't even going that fast. It's difficult to pedal hard when you're struggling to breathe. Something was seriously wrong with my ribs. Each breath felt like fire moving in and out of my lungs.

I wiped my brow with one arm while balancing with the other. I immediately noticed the red blotches on my blue jacket sleeve, the same arm I had just wiped my head with. Every part of my head and face stung. My vision blurred as I slowed even more. I had to get home and have my mother look at me. She was a nurse, so she could help.

"Chris!" Danielle pleaded again; her face hot with tears. "Please say something! I don't want you to be mad at me! I'm sorry!"

My mouth hurt too much to even try talking back, not that I would've known what to say. I counted my teeth with my tongue. Even though my mouth was full of blood, at least I didn't lose a tooth.

Danielle jumped off her bike to help me as I wobbled into my driveway. I stumbled off my bike and onto the pavement, Danielle trying to slow my fall as best she could.

"I'm so sorry..." she repeated. "It's all my fault."

I looked over at her, my cheek puffing out. She seemed confused as I turned her head with my hands and then patted her down.

"I'm okay," she whispered, realizing what I was doing. "You protected me. You did great!" She ran over and yelled through the open garage door for help.

"Jesus! Christopher! Are you okay?" I felt my mother's arms move around me and a searing pain erupted from my ribs as she hugged me. "I need to get him inside," she coldly said to Danielle.

"I'll help." Danielle said.

"No!" my mother snapped. "I think you've done enough. Go home, Danielle."

Tears ran down Danielle's face. "I'm so sorry!"

My mother gently led me inside. Danielle stood in the same spot, sobbing as our door forced her out. I smiled inside as I saw her before she disappeared. Not one scratch on her.

She was safe.

I did that.

• •

Earlier that morning, the sisters were fighting and bickering. At first, it was the normal spat between siblings that fizzled just as quickly as it began. But somehow, a lamp shattered while they went at it. Danielle's mom ran into the room and began cleaning what they left of it.

"Why don't you two just leave each other alone, for Christ's sake?" she erupted.

"What do you expect, Mom?" Michelle jawed back. "We're bored!"

"Go get your bikes and go outside!"

"I don't want to ride my bike," Michelle whined.

Their mom clenched her jaw and took a deep breath. "Fine. Danielle, you and Chris go out. Go. It's a beautiful day."

"Okay!" Danielle happily replied. She grabbed my hand and led me to a couple of dusty bikes in their garage. "Looks like you're riding Michelle's bike," she shrugged.

From behind the stack of rolled-up carpets, she wheeled out our rides. One was blue and the other pink. Each had a basket on its front with a white flower glued on. She rang one bell that latched onto the handlebars of each bike. A familiar *ring* filled the garage. She looked at me with a toothy grin.

I started backing away, my face contorted in confusion and aversion. I didn't expect the girls' bikes to be so... well, girly!

"Aw... come on!" she pleaded. With a twinkle in her eye, she added, "You'll look pretty on one of these!"

When I refused, she made a cute, mopey face.

"For me?"

She made her face even more of a caricature. It was then that I realized how weak I could be to the charms of a woman. Still, I loved her, and if it made her happy...

And did it ever! I, of course, got the pink bike. She went in circles around me, happily ringing her bell as we made our way to the end of Fairhaven.

"You're the best boyfriend *ever*!"

Whatever.

We made our way down Crocus Street and pedaled farther away from home. Back then, there was nothing but fields in that part of the neighborhood. Danielle stayed a little behind me, so I didn't know who she was talking to when I heard her yell, "Oh yeah? My boyfriend will kick your butt for that!"

That's when I noticed we weren't alone. Four boys we didn't recognize were riding their bikes nearby. At first, I paid little attention to them since they were still a considerable distance from us. But when I turned back to look at Danielle again, I saw her jerk her bike to a halt and jump off. She went after those boys like a rabid dog. I still don't know for sure what started it, but she was screaming at them at the top of her lungs.

"Hey you! Yeah, you! You jerk! My boyfriend will destroy you!" I could almost see foam forming around her mouth with how angry she had become. Next thing I knew, she was going full Chihuahua on them.

Among the four of them was a stocky kid who seemed like the leader of their pack. I'm pretty sure he was the one who made her angry, because she seemed focused on him. "Who? This kid? The boy with the flower bike?" he laughed viciously.

"It's okay. We don't want any trouble here," I said, trying to calm the situation. The last thing I wanted was a fight. My voice was barely audible over Danielle's endless yelling.

"I dare you to do that again!" she kept screaming.

By now, the two of us had ridden our bikes closer to their group. They were looking at each other, half-confused, half-amused. "Shut your ugly mouth or I'll knock your bitch ass out," the leader hollered back.

Damn it.

My temper flared. Everything tightened up. Blood rushed hot into all my muscles. *He thinks he's going to hurt her? Over my dead body.* I didn't care what could happen to me. All I cared about was her. The anger she expressed was now equal in me, simmering quietly. I was ready.

The leader violently ditched his bike to the side and stormed up to her, the others following suit, but I stepped in his way and pulled Danielle behind me.

I always knew that one day I would have to step up and protect her, and suddenly, here it was. Make no mistake, I was scared. But to my surprise, the fear did not paralyze me.

For a moment, I felt proud. *Is this what it feels like to be brave?* My mind flashed back to the memory of her dad walking me up the driveway just a few weeks earlier. I didn't protect Danielle then, but I was damn sure going to try now, even though I had no clue how to fight.

Boys, being a man is about defending what you love, even if it means getting hurt. Even if you are scared, you move forward. And that's exactly what I did. Almost instinctively, I moved forward, meeting him halfway into his charge.

SLAM! Our heads collided like two bulls testing each other. Each pushing with all his might to prove his dominance over the other. This brute kid snorted through his nose, spewing on about how he was going to kick my ass.

In a split second, our heads parted, and he hauled off and hit me square on the cheek. What I remember most is how little it hurt. *Maybe what Dad did to me prepared me for the real world*, I thought, almost amused.

"You want some more?" he asked as he positioned himself to strike again. I noticed myself smiling. This really wasn't that bad after all.

"Stop it!" Danielle screamed, grabbing at my shirt from behind. No way. I was the only thing keeping him from her.

He hit me again and again. I didn't care. I didn't budge. My treasure was behind me and I was protecting it. Even after hitting me as hard as he could, he couldn't get past me.

Minutes passed like this. I remember the look of shock on his face as I laughed off each hit. This kid hitting me felt like a gnat landing on my face compared to my old man. Then, I realized, there was no one threatening to kill my mother if I fought back. And I *could* fight back. That's when I heard an unknown voice in my head thunder: *KILL HIM! MAKE AN EXAMPLE OUT OF HIM! QUIT BEING WEAK AND DO IT YOU COWARD!*

Yet something held me back. It was an internal tug-of-war. One end of the rope showed that this guy was just like my dad. He had no problems hitting a woman. The other side argued that hitting back would mean I would be on my way to proving my mother right and turning into my father.

Each time I ate a shot, I became more frustrated with myself. I just stood there, getting punched in the face.

Hit him, you idiot! This is your moment!

Danielle screamed for help.

"Shut up, bitch! I'll get to you next!" he screamed back as he attempted to reach her again. He was coming within inches of hitting her. Inside, I was screaming. *YOU'RE LOSING! PUT HIM DOWN! IF YOU GET IN A FIGHT, BOY, YOU BETTER WIN!*

But I couldn't go through with it. My hands were in fists, but they wouldn't leave my sides. *I am not like my father. I am not like my father.*

As long as she was safe, that was all that mattered. Whatever happened to me was inconsequential. But I wasn't sure how much longer I could keep it up. My ears were ringing.

WHACK! Number eight made contact, but luckily this time, it was more of a paintbrush. Fatigue was setting in. My attacker was losing power. I knew he wouldn't last much longer.

"Do it again, harder this time!" I yelled at him. Adrenaline was keeping me together, keeping me engaged. His look of frustration turned to concern as he struggled to breathe.

Like a pack of hyenas, his friends tried sneaking over to Danielle. I lunged at them, which, once again, resulted in getting hit in the face, this time from one of his smaller friends.

I wasn't laughing anymore. Now it was really becoming serious. I had to stay focused. The more they advanced, the farther back I pushed her into the trees that lined the road. Finally, I felt her push back against me. We had reached the trees, and she had her back to one. Now I could handle all four of them.

Seeing this, their leader waved them off.

"Forget these losers!" he said. "Let's get out of here!" I don't remember if he was out of breath, gave up, or both. Danielle was sobbing behind me. I could feel her heaving against my back. I didn't move until I saw them disappear over the hill. It was over.

I went over to pick up my bike. It was then that the pain hit me like a sledgehammer. I felt like someone was poking my jaw with something hot. My nose stung. My adrenaline was flowing so much that I didn't even notice my eyes could barely open.

Danielle was crying as she tried touching me to comfort me. She apologized over and over, saying it was her fault. She blubbered she shouldn't have said anything to them, even though they were rude to me.

"I'm so sorry, Chris. Please don't be angry," she pleaded.

I was angry, but not at her. In fact, I had never felt so angry before in my life. It was the type of red-hot anger that could cause me to tear someone limb from limb without even realizing it, which was both exciting and frightening at the same time.

But why didn't I tear them apart? Why did I just stand there and take the abuse? There was no excuse. And now all that anger turned back in on me. I was weak, just like I was with my father. I hated that. Being powerless to hit back made me hate myself.

Danielle was now hugging me. She was still sobbing, but she was safe. They didn't hurt her. I was her human shield, and while my success gave me some slight comfort, my ego was furious that I didn't take those four out. Everyone needed to see that I could protect her. I wanted her to see that the other time with my father was a fluke. I could protect her. I *did* protect her! Her boyfriend took on four people by himself when they threatened her and she came out the other side without a scratch.

I had hoped she would tell her dad. Then he would see it, too.

• •

"You fought, didn't you?" my mother demanded. "You're just like your father!"

"Well, you're done with that girl," Dick chimed in.

Mom tried to hold me down as I leaned forward in the chair.

"I didn't fight. Danielle had nothing to do with it!" I yelled back.

"Hey!" he yelled back. "You want me to finish what they started?"

"Stop it, both of you!" Mom yelled. "He can still see Danielle until we leave. It's only a few more months, anyway."

"What? What are you talking about?"

"We're taking your father to court for full custody," she said. "That's why he was here the other day. We're leaving Florida in three months and moving to Michigan."

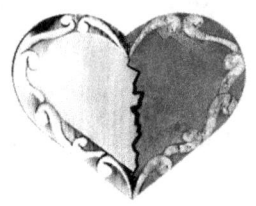

8

"That's Life"
(by Frank Sinatra)

I couldn't breathe. My vision blurred around my mother's face. Her mouth kept moving, but my ears kept ringing with the only word that mattered: leaving?

"No!" I yelled. "What do you mean, we're leaving?" Taken aback by the sudden tone in my voice, her hands went immediately to her hips, which was never a good thing.

"We're moving to Michigan. We have to take your father to court to make it happen, but it's happening. In three months we have the hearing, and after that, we're gone."

"But I don't want to move! I have too much here!"

"Like what?" she demanded.

"Friends," I said reluctantly after a moment's pause. Even I wasn't foolish enough to think it was true.

"You mean Danielle," she finished for me. I seethed with anger. *Yes, Mom, you're right, I have no friends.* Then she gave me the look. This was the look that told me I was only digging myself into a deeper grave by continuing forward with the conversation. I had gotten it before, but I'd never protested so loudly against it.

"I'm not talking about this with you anymore. We're leaving, and that's final."

With that, she turned and walked away, leaving me stunned in the middle of the hallway. Everything was falling apart in front of me. My life, this wonderful life, the answer to my prayers, was now being taken away from me.

I stormed into my room.

Over the next three months, I was ushered along an agonizing descent into hell. I was made into a pawn by my parents, a hostage held for use by both sides to spy, inquire, and inform. When spying wasn't enough, they instructed me to say certain things that one parent knew would set the other off. Both seemed to relish the reports I would give them that their plan to hurt the other was effective.

There were also lawyers. Each parent had their own who grilled me with questions that they knew would come up during the hearing. They were preparing me to testify before a judge and explain which parent I wanted to live with. They did not even consider Scott because he was almost twenty.

Meanwhile, since the same day he learned he was being taken to court, my father took on an entirely new character. All this time we'd lived on Fairhaven Street, we had spent every other weekend at my father's house for his visitations. He was the same as he ever was, but as long as we did what he said and stayed quiet, most weekends he just drank himself to sleep in front of the television. The violence was always in the background, and yes, he continued to use his hands and belt on us, but it wasn't as bad as those days before the divorce. Still, Scott and I hated him.

But after he learned I could testify against him in court, he started acting like a new man. The man stopped drinking. He stopped hitting us and putting us down. And he started being affectionate. I figured his lawyer must have had something to do with it since the change came after their first meeting. He'd put his arms around us from time to time, though we always winced when he did. He started saying "I love you" at random intervals, like he remembered it was on his to-do list for the day.

He also started making me promises that I could redeem if I lived with him after the hearing. As time passed, he would excitedly remind me of each one.

If I moved in with him, I wouldn't have to do chores. I wouldn't have a bedtime or a curfew if I went out. I could play video games if I wanted. He said he wanted to make amends for the way things were. Those things in the past were all my mother's fault anyway, according to him. If I gave him a chance, he would be the best dad ever and we could have fun every day.

Four years earlier, this would have been my dream come true, and for a time I even enjoyed it, or tried to. But in my heart was an unshakable doubt.

See boys, your grandfather could charm the pants off anyone. When he was sober, he was smooth with women and convincing with men. Now it was me he was trying to convince, pitching the idea that the risk of losing me woke him up and made him want to be a better man before it was too late. Of course, I wanted to believe it, but I knew him too well. Though I was too young to understand exactly what it was, I knew this sham transformation had an entirely different motivation.

There was another transformation, though, that was sincere without a doubt. For the first time, Scott was happy around dad. They started laughing and smiling, swapping stories and making jokes like a regular father and son. This was quite a contrast to the sullen, submissive behavior I was used to seeing from my brother. Scott couldn't look anyone in the eye after a beat down by dad.

Things improved so much that Scott did the unthinkable: He took my father up on his offer and moved in with him. On New Year's Eve, 1989, a few weeks before the court hearing, he and my mother had the fight of all fights when he threw his suitcase in the back of my father's truck. She screamed her head off, accusing him of betraying her. But off they went.

From that point on, the war between my parents escalated. Mom was no nonsense to me regarding the situation. She made no promises or attempts to persuade me, except that if I moved in with him, I wouldn't make it out alive.

"Remember what happened the last time he lived with us," she frequently insisted, as if I could ever forget. Over and over, she'd repeat her argument: "He doesn't care about you! Your father never cared about you, and he never will. He's just using you to hurt me."

Her strategy was to act as if she had all the cards, and I simply had no choice but to go with her. She showed no regret in plucking me from the home I loved. She offered no remorse for tearing me away from Danielle and certainly no compassion because moving away with her would mean ending my relationship with the only person who made me happy. Just as I could see how happy Scott was after Dad pretended to change, my mother had to have seen how happy I was after we moved to Fairhaven Street. How could she not care about taking that away from me? How could she not even talk to me about it?

Danielle didn't take the news well at all. After I told her, she changed as well. She was no longer the bubbly, vivacious girl I had always known. Her outgoing personality was now more reserved, almost melancholy. She became more affectionate, but in a clingy sort of way. She absolutely hated talking about my leaving, and she hated talking about my father even more.

If I tried to bring up the subject, her eyes would immediately fill with tears. She'd yell at me, telling me she didn't want to talk about it. Her nails were down to the cuticles because she bit them so much. It surprised me she even had any nail left. It was extremely painful for me to see her so upset, doubling the pain of my own feelings.

For all of this, I hated my mother. She was hurting Danielle, and I couldn't stand it. So, I decided I was going to do something about it. I marched back over to my house one day and stood behind my mother, who was at the kitchen sink.

"What are you looking at?" she asked while drying off a plate.

"You're hurting Danielle," I said brusquely.

She stopped what she was doing and turned to face me.

"How am I hurting her?"

"She's different now," I said. "She's been sad ever since you announced we were moving."

"I'm sorry to hear that," she said, resuming the dishes.

"No, you're not!" I belted out. She almost dropped the plate in her hands, but slowly placed it on the counter. She took a breath and faced me again.

"Excuse me, young man?"

"No. I don't think I will," I said, proud of the brashness and daring of my tone. "We don't have to move. You're just doing this because it's what you want. You want to get away from Dad."

"YES!" she shouted back. At least she was showing me some emotion. "Can you blame me?"

"Yes, I can blame you! You divorced him! You don't even have to deal with him anymore. He's our problem. But you want revenge. You love to see how much this is pissing him off! And you don't even care about how much this is hurting me and Danielle!"

"I don't like your tone." she said, lowering her brow and her voice.

"You didn't even ask me how I felt about moving," I said as calmly as I could manage.

"Because I knew how you would feel. You would've blown up about your little girlfriend, just like you are now."

"You're tearing us apart!" I shouted. "And you don't even care about it! I bet you didn't even consider it!"

"Us?" she said, throwing a towel on the counter. "Us? Let me tell you something, mister. There is no 'us' with the two of you. You two aren't even dating!"

"Yes, we are!"

"No, you're not! You're too young to date!"

"We love each other!"

"Love?" she laughed. "What do you know about love? You're thirteen!"

What do I know about love? I was smoking with rage. *I know more about love than you!*

I was right, too. I had experienced more love at thirteen than my mother had ever known. But I was too angry to feel the sadness of that realization, then.

"Christopher," she continued, hands on her hips again, "what you are experiencing is puppy love. It's not real. The two of you are nothing serious. Danielle will move on with someone else within a week of our leaving. I hate to break it to you, but she never loved you. You'll be forgotten like yesterday's news. And anyway, you'll move on too once we get to Michigan."

"THIS ISN'T FAIR!" I screamed in desperation. *Danielle is my soul mate. There is no moving on from that!*

"Well, what can I tell you? Life isn't fair. Didn't you learn that from everything your father put us through? It wasn't fair that he beat the shit out of me day in and day out for a decade. It isn't fair that I still have to deal with his bullshit, yet here I am drowning in it! I'm tired of putting up with him. I did the best I could to raise the two of you by myself. I sacrificed for you two, and your brother screws me over. And don't you dare screw me over, too. You owe me!"

I bit the inside of my cheeks to stop myself from speaking. I was afraid if I screamed anymore, I might lose control.

"You are a child. You will do as you are told. And I'm telling you to make the right decision. Either you come with us to Michigan and have a nice new life, or you can go live with your father until he beats you dead and throws your body in a ditch. That's your choice."

"Is this how you act like you care about me? Maybe I will just move in with Dad!"

"Go ahead! It's your funeral," she said flippantly. Then, in a nasty voice, she added, "Grow the hell up."

I realized she was right. I had to face a whole new level of growing up.

Would I stay with my abusive father, hoping I could simultaneously continue my storybook romance with the first girl I'd ever loved, or would I go with my mother, leave the abuse, and leave my soul mate behind?

• •

As the weeks passed, prep for the hearing intensified. The lawyers became less tolerant if I incorrectly parroted the answers they'd coached me to give. I was horrible at memorizing lines like this, and it was twice as hard because I had two different scripts. My mother expected me to tell the judge how abusive my father was and that I wanted to live with them. My father expected me to tell the judge that he had never abused me and that my mother was a liar and just out to get him.

One day my dad's lawyer got so fed up with me not answering the question to his liking, he told my father about it. Dad came over and pulled me to the side. I was sure he was going to hit me.

But he didn't. Instead, he rubbed my back.

"Seems like you're having a hard time with the questions, son," he said, directing me out the back door. The two of us went out to the dock on the river that ran through his backyard. We fed the ducks as he poked and prodded more about what was going on.

"I just don't want to mess up," I told him, lying through my teeth. The ducks were swimming by as I looked down. I didn't want to test how far this new-and-improved version of my dad would stretch.

"Look," he said, turning to me, "as long as you go in there and tell the truth, nothing bad is going to happen. Just tell the judge what really happened, and I'll be proud of you. I promise."

I looked up at him. He looked sincere.

Maybe he had changed after all?

But I had no desire to live with him. I wanted to live with Danielle and her family. That's where my genuine family was. The people who I belonged with always cared about me, accepted me, included me, and never tried to manipulate me.

Even if I stayed in Florida with him, he lived a twenty-minute drive from Fairhaven Street. Would I be able to see Danielle at all?

Fat chance.

I didn't want either parent. I wanted to be grown up and in a house of my own, where Danielle could fall asleep in my arms every night, her grandmother's engagement ring still on her finger. But it didn't matter what I wanted. I only had two options.

9

"Integrity Blues"
(by Jimmy Eat World)

I had no appetite when I awoke the next morning. The butterflies slamming into the walls of my stomach killed any desire to eat. Despite my mother's complaints, I just sat at the breakfast table, trying to ignore the thick blanket of tension that had moved over us.

Reluctantly, I dressed in a plain white dress shirt with a candy-cane-striped tie. I hated ties because they always felt like they were choking me. But today the tie wasn't the only thing that made me feel like I was choking.

If I stayed in Florida, it would mean that my mother would lose to my father, something she'd been constantly reminding me of over the last week or so. She'd become obsessed with winning in court. Even at such a young age, I could see where I was in the packing order when it came to her priorities.

The car ride over to the courthouse was agonizing. The entire time she droned on about how she couldn't wait to leave Florida, about how she was owed this for everything he did, about how she was going to win. She was going to rub it right in his face.

I just leaned on the back door to tune her out. I rested my elbow against the car window as I watched people move about their lives. They all seemed so happy, able to make their own decisions, control their own lives. *I wonder what that's like.*

My mother broke my daydream as she snapped her fingers to get my attention. "Chris, we've been preparing you for months, so just say the right thing and it will be over quickly."

The right thing for you, maybe. I'm getting screwed in the worst way, and no one even acknowledges it. Not a word about what I have to give up so you can get what you want.

After a ten-minute lecture on the impact of lies on the lives of other people, we finally arrived. I just wanted to get out of that car as quickly as possible.

They led me into the building and through a series of corridors until we reached the main hallway right outside the courtroom. It was a long, yellow hallway with small chandeliers hanging along its length. I looked up at the one above us, hoping it would fall and hit me so I couldn't go through with what I had to do next.

They instructed me to sit down on a bench situated right in front of the entry to the courtroom. The entry was closed with two heavy, wooden double doors that hissed when they opened. From where I sat, they looked like they were nine feet tall.

"Do the right thing," Dick said coldly, pointing his finger in my face as he opened the door. He allowed my mother through, and the doors slowly swallowed them until they were out of sight.

I looked to my left as I heard one of the side doors open. Out stepped my father, his wife, Gail, and Scott. They walked up to me, my father smiling. He reached over and touched me on the shoulder.

Scott wouldn't even look at me. Sullen and submissive, his head was down as he dutifully walked by. I knew what that meant. He followed them and the doors swallowed them up.

A nearby clock ticked. The hallway was silent, except for that sound, which to my ears was as loud as a cannon blast. I felt like I was awaiting execution.

I really don't want to go to jail, I thought. *I'd never see Danielle again!*

This fear was another gift from Dad's lawyer, who'd told me the week before when I failed to say what he wanted me to. "Remember, son," he bellowed, "perjury is a crime. If you lie under oath, you can go to jail."

I jumped at the sudden click of a doorknob. A side door I hadn't noticed opened, and an older woman with round glasses and gray and black hair popped her head out.

"The judge is ready for you."

I looked at her, scared and confused. I thought I was going into the courtroom. *Why do they want to see me behind closed doors? Is it so it's easier to take me away in handcuffs without making a scene?*

Reluctantly, I rose and followed her.

She led me down another long hallway, this one with offices sprinkled throughout. We continued until we reached the last door at the very end. Stopping in front of it, she glared at me before lightly knocking.

A voice boomed from the other side. "Enter."

The woman opened the door and slid in.

"Mr. Smith is here to see you, Your Honor."

"Send him in."

She turned and opened the door wider for me. I saw an office bigger than our living room. Rows of thick, dusty books sat on tall bookcases that ran along every wall.

In the center of the room was a thick wooden desk with one chair behind it and two in front. The chair back was facing away from us as I entered. I could just make out what appeared to be white hair over the top of the main chair.

Excusing herself, the woman exited the room, carefully closing the door behind her.

"Sit down, young man," the judge said, still not revealing his face.

I quickly did as I was instructed. I wasn't messing with anyone who could send me to jail. Just as I sat down, his chair turned around to face me.

He was an old man, his hair carefully coiffed. Bifocals sat on the end of his nose. He put a medium-sized binder on the desk in front of him and slowly flipped through the pages.

"Do you prefer to be called Chris?" he asked. "Or C.J.?" I immediately shook my head no once I heard "C.J."

"Do you know why you are here, Chris?"

"My mom wants to move to Michigan, and she can't take me with her unless she gets your permission."

He smiled. "That's true. But there's more to it than that." He leaned back in his chair slightly as he continued. "I've already talked with your mother and father," he said. "And I heard two very different stories from two very different people. Their lawyers have done a good job preparing them. So, before I can decide, I need more information. I'm hoping to get that from you."

I swallowed hard.

"You seem nervous, son."

I could only nod in response. He leaned in, putting his arms on the desk.

"What's going on?"

I sat there for a moment, weighing my options for what I was going to say next. He didn't seem mean, but then again, he didn't seem nice either. I looked around his desk, noticing all the papers and files neatly organized. My eyes went around until I reached a hammer-looking thing on the far right.

"Know what that is?" he asked, motioning toward it.

"No, sir."

"It's a gavel. I use it when I'm talking to people and deciding cases. It sits on a small block of wood, and when I want to get a person's attention or make an official decision, I signify it by hitting that block of wood with that gavel."

I blinked. "You don't hit people with it?"

His eyebrows raised as he let out a small chuckle.

"No, I don't hit people with it," he said. "Though I will admit, it can be tempting with the people I deal with. But I don't hit anyone with it because no one ever deserves to be hit."

I slowly nodded, still hesitant to say anything else.

"Do you know what my job is, Chris?"

I looked back up at him. "You put people in jail?"

He chuckled again. "Not all the time, but sometimes, yes. If they committed a crime, then yes, I put them in jail. Are you afraid I'll do that to you?"

I nodded again.

"Who told you that might happen?"

"My dad's lawyer. He said if I lied, I would go to jail."

His joking demeanor stopped almost immediately. "He shouldn't have told you that. Were you thinking about lying to me?"

I shook my head no. "I don't know what to say, sir."

"What do you mean?" he asked.

With a gigantic sigh and a small voice, I explained to him that the lawyers had been riding me hard to say what they wanted me to say. I could see him tense up. He was obviously becoming angry; I was just hoping it wasn't at me.

"I'm sorry you're going through all of this," he said after I finished. "You shouldn't be in this position. As I was saying before, my job is more than putting people in jail. My job is to solve problems. The problems I solve are those like the one your parents are fighting about right now."

He got up and came to sit next to me, turning the chair to face me.

"I'm not here to hurt you, Chris, or anyone. I only need to know the truth. I need to know the *actual* truth, not what you rehearsed. Just tell me what you've been through, what happened when your parents lived together. And before you tell me, I want you to know something. I deal with young people like you every day. Some have parents who hit them or threaten to hurt them if they tell me what really happens at home."

He leaned in and took a deep breath.

"I think maybe you're in a situation like this, hmm? And if you are, I can stop your dad from ever hurting you or your mom ever again. I can help you, that's my job, but you must tell me the truth. So, I don't want you to be afraid, okay? You take your time, and when you are ready, just tell me what's going on. Okay?"

He got back up and returned to his seat. He turned around until he was facing away from me, an effort to help me feel comfortable.

I sat in silence for a few minutes, my head swimming with thoughts: *Mom couldn't care less about what I'm giving up to give her what she wants. All she cares about is winning, even when I'm losing everything. And I want to believe Dad has changed. Scott said nothing about regretting his decision to move in with him. But I saw the way he looked today. But maybe if I'm there, too, I can help this new dad stick. I want Dad to be proud of me. At least he knows how to act like he cares. All Mom cares about is getting what she feels she's owed. And I don't want to leave Danielle. And she doesn't want me to leave. I love her so much. She was the answer to my prayers. If God brought me and Danielle together, how could it be right that I leave her now? Dad promised I could see her whenever I wanted. But I'd be stupid to believe that! He lives all the way in Melbourne! I'd need Dad to drive me, and he won't even take me bowling! And what happens if I stay with him and he goes back on all his promises, and Mom's already gone. What if he kills me?*

My eyes wandered to the empty chair next to me, and suddenly I saw Danielle sitting there. She was so real. Her left hand was on my leg. I could see her grandmother's engagement ring loosely around her finger. It was like I could reach out and touch her. She was smiling at me, and it was calming.

I wasn't alone. The way she looked at me, I knew no matter what happened, I would never be alone again.

It was going to be okay.

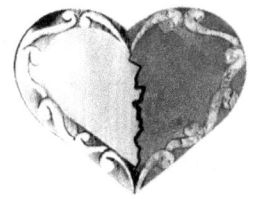

10

"You're Gonna Get What's Coming"
(by Robert Palmer)

I could feel every eye pierce through me as I was escorted into the courtroom, led by the lady from before. There had to have been at least twenty people sitting in the audience, most of whom I did not recognize.

I had never been in a courtroom before, only ever seeing them on television. Watching *L.A. Law* could never have prepared me for just how intimidating this was.

The room was bigger than our house and quiet as a tomb, save the occasional whisper. A curved mahogany barrier wrapped around half the room, dividing those there on business and those just observing.

In the center of the barrier was a swivel door. Pushing it open, I walked carefully to the first row of the spectator section behind my mother and stepfather. My job was done. I was now an observer.

The chair I approached was upholstered in red vinyl that released an embarrassing squeal as I sat down. The sound echoed throughout the court, and I could feel all eyes on me again, disapproving, condemning me.

I tried shifting my weight. I just wanted to get comfortable, to find the slightest relief in this experience, but even that was forbidden. Only by sitting perfectly still and upright could I do what they expected of me.

Still like a statue, frozen in place, I looked over at the first row of spectator chairs behind my father and Gail, on my right. Scott was situated right behind Dad, his hands in his lap. Sensing my stare, he looked over at me. Attempting silent communication, he mouthed his question: *What did you say?*

I just shrugged, hoping the judge would come out soon with his verdict. Noticing our attempts at covert communication, my mother's lawyer whipped around and gave me a sharp look. She held a finger to her lips. I returned my eyes to the front.

The clock ticked away as we waited. After hundreds, maybe thousands of ticks had passed, my dad's lawyer checked his watch in frustration and whispered something to his client. Dad then turned his head to look at me. The look on his face mirrored what Scott had been asking.

Again, I just shrugged. My father's face grew more concerned. The tension in the room was heavy. I returned to the fearful, frozen posture of a helpless boy. I hated it.

"ALL RISE," the bailiff suddenly bellowed. Everyone shot up to their feet. My mother gripped Dick's hand like a vise.

The door opened, and the judge appeared. He walked up the two steps leading to his bench.

"Be seated," he commanded. We sat. I shifted over to the next seat, cushioned with fabric, so I made no more noise.

The judge took a moment to get comfortable. He placed in front of him the same binder he was looking through with me, scanning the audience with dispassionate eyes, a scowl draped across his face. This was not the same friendly person I had gotten to know in the office in the back.

He took his bifocals off and placed them on the table in front of him.

"I've been a judge for thirty years," he began. "I see many people come and go. They all have their own stories, their own problems. Some are decent people. Innocent people. I very much want to help these people and I do the best I can to do so."

"Then there are others who are not such good people. These people make my job very challenging."

He then leaned forward, turning to my father.

"You, sir, are an example of that latter person."

My father's face turned ashen gray.

"I know I kept all of you in suspense, and that was for good reason. I've been presiding for a long time now. But in this case, I needed the extra time to make sure I could keep my composure when I addressed you, sir."

He took another pause.

"Normally, I pride myself on being professional, but this one really hit close to home for me. Sir, I have been blessed with four children who, fortunately, have grown up to become sound, capable adults. I also have three grandchildren who are well on their way to becoming like their parents."

"I am not one to brag," he continued, "but a big part of the reason my kids turned out so well was because I loved them at home. I didn't yell at them, I didn't scream at them, and I certainly *never hit them*."

My father's face had a mixture of confusion and rage.

"I had a very disturbing conversation with your son. I had a feeling from talking to you about what he was going to say and was shocked by what he told me. The things that have happened to both young men, the things that they have witnessed while under your care, make me sick. If I could do it now, I'd put you in prison and let you rot for the rest of your life. It would give me great pleasure."

I looked over at Scott, who was now glaring at me. I could see the fear in his eyes. *What did you do?* he mouthed.

Dad's eyebrows were furrowed now, his jaw clenched. His lawyer touched him on the shoulder to calm him. I knew that was like touching the door to a room on fire. My father turned toward me with furious eyes.

"Hey!" the judge yelled, "You look at *me* when I'm talking to you, do you understand? You don't look at him. I'm the one talking."

My father's lips moved. He was muttering under his breath. The judge's sudden challenge cut through the momentary silence like a chainsaw.

"Is there something your client would like to say?"

His lawyer whispered to him, but my father was already beginning to boil over.

"Let him talk!" the judge commanded. "He clearly has something he wants to say. But allow me to caution you, sir, choose your next words carefully."

His lawyer backed off, concerned. My father's hands were now tightly clenched as he tried to find restraint.

"I *never* hit either of my children or my ex-wife! Clearly, she's the one who—"

"We both know that is not true, sir," the judge interrupted.

"This is BULLSHIT!"

The judge stood up. "Excuse me! You are not to speak in such a manner in my courtroom. Is that understood?"

"You can't do anything to me. This is bullshit. I'm going home." He turned, grabbed his things in one hand, Gail in the other, and began storming toward the main entrance to the courtroom.

Smacking the top of his stand, the judge shot again to his feet and let out a bellow that caused everyone in the courtroom to flinch.

"YOU WILL RETURN TO YOUR SEAT NOW, OR I WILL HOLD YOU IN CONTEMPT!"

My father stopped in his tracks. He continued to face the door. You could see the wheels turning in his head as he briefly weighed his options.

"There are police officers right outside that door. I've already instructed them to assist my bailiff in taking you into custody if you made a scene. I promise you, sir, if you attempt to leave this building before I say you can, you will not make it past that door." Then, addressing my father's lawyer, he added, "You! Go get your client before he does something stupid!"

The lawyer scurried to my father's side. After a few moments of muffled back-and-forth, my father released Gail and turned. He turned and slowly sauntered down the aisle back to his seat. Gail followed, shaking her arm and rubbing it.

"Are you okay, ma'am?" the judge asked. Gail quickly nodded and sat down. Picking up his gavel, the judge turned his attention back toward my father.

"Do you know what your son asked me about my gavel? First question out of his mouth. Can you guess?"

My father didn't respond.

"He thought I hit people with it. Why do you think that is?"

"I don't know," my father snapped back. "My son is not too smart."

The judge's face turned bright red.

"I've only known Chris for an hour, and I know he is far more intelligent than you. There is only one reason a young man his age would immediately assume it was a weapon, and that is because all he has known in his life is violence. Violence that you perpetrated."

I couldn't believe it. My father, the self-proclaimed unstoppable force, was silent. This stranger, this old man who looked like he couldn't fight off a cold, had put him in his place.

There was no way dad could fight back. Earlier, when I told him all the dark and shameful secrets of our house and our family, I feared it might be for nothing. I was afraid that the judge didn't have any power to help us. Now I saw I was completely wrong. This guy had some serious power. I was in awe as he continued to dress down my father.

"While this was one of the hardest cases I've had to get through, one upside was that the decision was easy to make."

My father swallowed hard as the clock kept ticking in the background.

"Ms. Hudson, it is the decision of this court that you are to be granted permission to take Christopher to Michigan with you. He himself has decided to stay with you and your husband."

Turning back to my father, whose head was bowed in shame, he said, "Sir, I am utterly disgusted with you. If you ever appear before me in this courtroom again, I swear I will make an example out of you."

The judge pointed at me. "I have given this young man my personal phone number. I'm extending that information to your eldest as well. If you lay a hand on either of them or your ex-wife again, I give them express permission to call me immediately anytime, day or night. If I ever receive a call, you have my word that I will see to it you never see the light of day again. Is that understood?"

"Yes, Your Honor," his lawyer responded.

"And *you*," the judge added, pointing at the lawyer. "Did you tell Christopher that he would go to jail if he didn't say what you wanted him to say?"

"Uh, no, Your Honor, that's not what I said."

"Don't you lie to me!"

The lawyer cleared his throat. "I only aimed to educate the child about perjury, Your Honor. "

"Why don't I believe that? I want to see you in my chambers after this."

The judge looked at me with raised eyebrows, holding up the gavel to get my attention. With a swift movement of his hand, it came crashing down on the block of wood. *BANG!*

"*That* is what it's used for. We are adjourned."

He rose and made his way back through the same door he came from. I watched him go as if he were God Himself.

For so long, I wanted to know how I could finally protect my family. Not only protect my family but protect others who were in similar situations as well. I had always thought the only way to do that was through violence. But here I'd learned there was another way.

It was my calling. I could stop people like my father. Nothing bad would ever happen to us again if I were a judge.

A sudden rush of wind stirred me from my daze. My father blasted past me with Gail and Scott in tow. Scott looked back at me. I had never seen him so frightened before in my life. No doubt my father was going to take it out on him when they got home. My stomach sank with guilt. By telling the truth, I had put my brother in danger as well.

After they disappeared, I looked over at my mother, who was hugging Dick.

"I won. I'm free!" She was elated as she sobbed on his shoulder. I watched from my chair behind them as they celebrated their big win. They did not thank me, nor did they hug me. They didn't even turn to look at me.

I had simply done my job, done what I was told to do, and given my mother what she felt she deserved. They were happy. I tried to take comfort in knowing I had done the right thing, but was it really the right thing? I had told the truth, but what would it cost me? And what would it cost my brother?

As I stood there, alone, my imagination brought me a vision. It was me up on that bench, wearing the same robe as that judge, banging my gavel to punish bullies and wife-beaters. Then I saw myself walking through the door of a big, beautiful house. I took off my robe and embraced two little children who ran into my arms. Danielle was there behind them, so proud of the man I had become. I was powerful, victorious, and free to live my life with the woman I loved.

That's when the pit in my stomach dropped to the floor.

Danielle! *What have I done?*

11

"No Son of Mine"
(by Genesis)

Her parents would have to drag me out of my clothes to get me to leave. With everything falling apart, I knew where I belonged. But when we got home, they were nowhere to be found. Their house was dark, their driveway empty.

I waited on their front porch. Sitting in the heat, my shirt was quickly soaked through with sweat. I needed to see her, to be near her before I burst from missing her. I waited for hours. The sun set as the mosquitoes quickly found me. But I didn't care. I didn't move until my mother called out and made me go home.

The next morning, I leapt out of bed to look out my window. Still nothing. All day I stayed glued to that window until, at last in the early evening, their car pulled into the driveway. I raced over, meeting them as they went into the house. Danielle gave me a quick hug and led me inside.

We went to her bedroom and crashed on the floor. I told her every detail about what had happened. She listened eagerly, lovingly, as she had always listened to me before. She even withheld her comments, intuitively understanding how badly I just needed to get the weight of the courtroom events off my chest. That was, until I told her the worst part.

"I have one last weekend with him."

Her eyes doubled in size. "Why? He'll kill you!"

"I know," I responded, not even trying to hide my frustration. "And my mom is insisting I go."

"I don't get it. She won. Why would she make you go? She made you testify against him in court, and now she sends you to his house, alone? Why? He'll kill you! Don't go!"

Her eyes began watering. I felt guilty for dragging her through these emotions.

"I don't have a choice. I tried telling her all that, but she just said, '*You have the judge's number.*'"

Danielle grabbed me and hugged me tight, sniffling in my ear. She was trying desperately to keep it together and failing. "I don't know how much more of this I can take," she said, her voice breaking, "It's bad enough you're leaving, but to add... It's not fair!"

Hearing her so upset was like a knife to the gut.

It was going to be a long week, during which even Gail tried to convince my mother that going to my dad's was a bad idea. But my mother said it was a court-ordered visitation and that Gail should mind her own business. The day came, a Saturday, and he showed up to get me.

Danielle waited at her front door until she saw his truck pull up. Her dad refused to let her go to my house.

Gail jumped out instead and waited while I threw my suitcase in the bed and got in the passenger side. She didn't even look at me.

Fifteen long minutes later, we pulled up to their house. She parked the truck quickly and stormed into the house. "Grab your crap and get inside," she said as she disappeared.

I stood in front of the house, looking at the open door in front of me. I'd felt uncomfortable there before, especially when I was warned of Dad's foul mood, but this was different. The feeling I had that day went beyond discomfort.

If I go in there, I might never come back out.

I jabbed my hand in my pocket and felt the flimsiness of the paper in there, the one with the judge's phone number on it. This was my protection? Where my father lived, the nearest neighbor was almost two miles away. The only phone, if I needed it, was through that door.

Upon entering, my feelings intensified when I noticed his Beretta was not on the kitchen table where it normally was. If Dad was out and about, his gun was on him. If he was home, it stayed on that table unless he was about to use it. His other truck was at the house when we got home, so he had to have been in the house somewhere.

Hearing the TV in the living room near me, I poked my head around the corner cautiously to see where everyone was. Two recliners faced the TV on the far wall. Gail had sat down in one of them, half-turned away from me. In the other, turned completely away from me, I saw my father's balding head.

At first, I thought he was asleep since he didn't seem to move, but his hand suddenly moved over to the stand next to his chair. He grabbed for something, and my eyes widened in terror as I saw his hand go over the Beretta.

"Can I get you something to eat, honey?" Gail asked.

He let out a belch. "Yeah, sounds good."

Gail shot a nasty look at me, as if warning me to stay away. I knew the only way to get through the weekend was to be as invisible as possible. If I could just keep a low profile in my bedroom, sneaking out only when it was necessary, maybe I'd survive.

For the next twenty-four hours, I stayed in that little room, which had no toys or games or anything else to help me pass the time. I just sat there, my senses all on high alert, registering every little noise from the hallway, every throat-clearing, every shuffle of feet.

That evening, I heard Dad go into the kitchen. I kept an ear to the door, waiting for him to make his way back to the living room. But I heard the footsteps grow louder, nearer. I ran over to my bed and ducked under the covers, holding my breath and pretending to be asleep. The doorknob turned.

His stare burned a hole through my blankets. I could see him so clearly in my mind, looking at me, weighing his options for what he could get away with. I could see the gun in his hand, finger on the trigger. In my mind, I could see him grab the pillow, put it over my head, point the gun, and pull the trigger. As far as Gail and Scott were concerned, I deserved it. I betrayed my father, and no one does that and gets away with it.

The door closed again, and I let out an exhale of relief. Half of the weekend was done. I had only Sunday to endure.

• •

Sunday wasn't much better. But I knew I was due home at 5:00 p.m., and with any luck Gail would be the one to take me home and I would never have to see any of them again. Just a few more hours of vigilant silence, and I'd be free.

By 4:00 p.m. I'd already packed my things—my pajamas and toothbrush—and was ready to go. If Gail agreed to drive me, I would live. Unfortunately, it was around this time that the silence that had engulfed the house all weekend ceased when Dad and Gail burst into an argument.

"I'm not taking him!" Dad yelled.

"You have to," Gail shouted back, "I can't take him because I have an appointment."

I heard the familiar sounds of scuffling, followed by Gail apologizing repeatedly. "I'm sorry you're mad, honey, but I just can't do it." She sounded like someone in physical pain. "Look, you just get him home and we'll be done with it, okay?"

Objects were being slammed on the kitchen table. Would he put up his gun, or take it with him? I prayed he might be so angry that it would simply slip his mind.

But there was little doubt that he had it. And I was about to spend twenty minutes in a car with him.

Gail's head popped into the bedroom. "Time to go. Grab your shit. Your father is taking you, so keep your mouth shut if you know what's good for you."

He didn't make a single sound throughout the trip. There was no yelling, no screaming, no threats, just silence and the smoke of Pall Mall cigarettes washing over me. His gun was on his right hip instead of his left. I didn't know what to make of that.

Finally, we pulled onto Fairhaven Street. I could see my house in the distance. Almost home. I was so close to finally being free. It didn't matter if everything that happened hurt his feelings. I didn't care if he hated me. I didn't care if I never saw him again. All I cared about was getting out of that car.

He pulled over to the side of the street, just halfway down Fairhaven toward our house, and put the truck into park. We just sat there, both looking ahead. I did not know what was about to happen, but I kept my hand close to the release of the car door.

I could see the gun in my peripheral vision. His hand wasn't touching it, but it was close. If he tried to grab it, I would go for the lever and try to get out as fast as I could. He still had to pull the gun from the holster and chamber a round before he could shoot, which seemed like just enough time to make a break for the house, or at least the nearest neighbor.

I jumped at the sudden sound of his voice. "Your mother and I were talking about you coming over for the summer."

I looked over at him, petrified. "But because you lied about me in court, I don't think that's such a good idea anymore."

My brow lowered. My nostrils flared. I was shocked to find my fear being replaced with anger. He kept talking, growing louder and angrier as he went on about how I betrayed him, how me and my mother were both liars.

My voice came as a surprise to me. "I don't care!" I said, almost as loudly as him. "I didn't lie! You hit us! I watched you beat Mom unconscious the last day you lived with us! You almost killed her!"

A vein bulged from my father's forehead. If there ever was a time when he was going to kill me, this was it. But I didn't think about that in this moment. I was tired of fearing him. "If you want to kill me, get it over with. I have nothing left to live for, anyway."

His hand jerked toward his weapon. I grabbed the door handle and pulled, but it wouldn't open. He'd put on the child safety lock.

"You want to leave?" he growled between curled lips. He pushed the button that released the lock. I jumped out of the car as fast as I could.

"One last thing before you go," he said calmly. I don't know why I didn't run, but I didn't. Through the window, I glared at him, boldly breaking his rule against looking him in the eye. He looked back at me, pointed his finger, and said, "You will never amount to anything. You're weak and pathetic and you always will be. Your brother, he'll go places in life. You? You're just a lying piece of shit. Walk the rest of the way home. Go to Michigan and never come back."

With a last blow of smoke in my face, he sped off. While it was hardly surprising, it still felt like a dagger to the heart. As anyone who's been abused can tell you, verbal abuse can hurt just as bad as physical.

When the two of you were born, I vowed to never speak meanly to you, even when you made me upset. I know I'm not a perfect father, but I will die happy knowing I never spoke to my kids the way my father spoke to me. To this day, he still claims I'm lying about the abuse against me, despite over twenty years of counselors telling me I am a textbook child abuse survivor and my brother being a witness to it.

What my father didn't realize, or care about, was that every single time he hit me or my mom or my brother, every time he put me down, it was like adding a gallon of gas to a fuel tank inside me. By the time we left for Michigan, his disowning me had just lit a match, causing an explosion that he would deal with years down the line when we would see each other again.

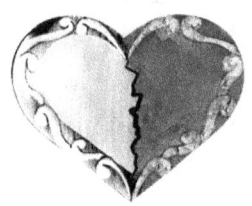

12

"Diamonds and Pearls"
(by Prince and the New Power Generation)

In the days leading up to our departure from Fairhaven Street, my mother decided that we would make one last "goodbye tour" with all our friends in the area. Since I didn't have any friends other than Danielle, I asked that we go visit Dad's mom, your great-grandmother, one last time.

Grandma Leona was my favorite person in my life, second only to Danielle, of course. We had a special bond, one that my brother was frequently jealous of. Since the day I was born, Grandma always gravitated toward me, or at least that was what Scott said.

As I got older, I felt comfortable telling her anything and everything, and I did. We would keep in touch with each other over the phone, and she was the first to hear about a lot of the things that happened in my life.

She was a God-fearing woman and a hopeless romantic. I'm certain I got my romantic side from her. That day of my first kiss, the first person I told was Grandma Leona. I knew the story 'd thrill her. She always swore to me that one day I would meet the girl of my dreams.

On the day of the kiss, I ran home and snuck the kitchen phone into my bedroom so I could call her. The coiled rubber phone cord stretched to its limit. You might think my mother would've thought this was cute, but she didn't. She didn't have a great relationship with my father's mother, mostly because Grandma always defended her son's indefensible behavior.

She'd always make excuses for him: he's tired, he's stressed, he has more on his plate than we realize. Eventually, I learned how his own father abused him as a child. But according to Grandma, he was just misguided. She had nothing but sympathy for her son, and she resented my mother for giving up on the marriage. "We don't give up on those we love," she said, scoldingly. After that point, my mother refused to talk to her and saw her as delusional.

"Hi, C.J.!" Grandma squealed on the phone, her usual greeting. She was the only person I tolerated calling me C.J.

"Hi, Grandma, guess what?" I said excitedly. "I had my first kiss!"

She gasped in amazement. "See, hon, I told you you would find someone special one day! Is it that Danielle who you were telling me about?"

"Yep!"

"Aw, I am so proud of you!" she said gleefully.

"There's one more thing."

She gasped again, slightly.

"What?"

"I think we're boyfriend and girlfriend now."

"Oh, that's wonderful," she said. "And I'm not surprised you have yourself a girlfriend already. You are a handsome young man, after all."

"I'm really not, Grandma," I half-laughed.

"Yes, you are!" she said. "And Danielle's got good taste if she latched onto you. I have a good feeling about this. I bet she's the one I told you about! The girl of your dreams, isn't she? Did you pray about it?"

Grandma always had a good feeling about things. A true optimist, she was the only person to plant in my head the idea that one day I would find an amazing girl, and when I did, I'd know it. Back then, I thought she was just trying to cheer me up when the other kids were picking on me. But she was right.

Grandma Leona was your stereotypical grandmother: four foot ten, wrinkled face with pronounced cheeks, and short, white, curly hair that resembled the coat of a poodle. She always wore flower-printed dresses and a pearl necklace and smelled like Icy Hot and chocolate chip cookies.

One of the greatest memories I have of her was us laying on her couch, watching one of her old black-and-white romance movies. My head was in her lap, and she was stroking my hair and humming softly. She frequently told me she thought I had the most beautiful brown hair she had ever seen. I thought of her every time I'd stroke your hair when we watched TV.

Grandma loved classic romantic movies like *Casablanca* and *Meet Me in St. Louis*. She had a massive collection of romance novels. She was a sucker for a good love story and dreamed of being in one. I like to think about how overjoyed she would be if she knew I would grow up to live her dream and capture it within the pages of my own book.

"True love never dies," she'd say. Having the exact opposite ideas of my mother, she also believed, "When you're young, you feel it even stronger. Young love is the truest love of all."

So the day I went to see her for the last time before moving was not one I looked forward to. She and Danielle were the women in my life, and I was about to leave them both. Grandma greeted me with her usual gentle bear hug, kissing me on the head repeatedly.

"How are you?" she asked.

I was near tears.

"Oh, honey," she said, hugging me again, "It's going to be okay."

"It's just... everything!" I sniffled. "I'm leaving everything I love. I'm leaving you and I'm leaving Danielle! My father disowned me and thought I was a liar!"

Grandma's jaw tensed.

"I'm sorry, honey," she said. "He shouldn't have done that. I know it's hard to see now, but he really didn't mean it. He was upset. You know how he gets."

I pulled away from her with a sudden jerk. "Why do you keep standing up for him?"

She looked at me, startled. Her blind devotion reminded me of someone else I knew and loved. "Because he's my son, and I love him just like I love you. You don't give up on people you love."

I was tempted to argue, but it wasn't worth it. I knew this was my last day with her and I didn't want to ruin it. If she'd stand up for him on the days we showed up with bruises and blood on our clothes, today would not be any different.

"Come back and sit by me, sweetie," she coaxed. I complied, and she put her arm around me. "With Danielle, remember what I've always told you. Everything happens for a reason. There are no such things as accidents. The two of you are meant to be."

We sat there together like that on her love seat for a few heavy moments, a hot Florida breeze coming through the screen door, until a familiar smell filled my nose. Chocolate chip cookies. She always knew how to diffuse a situation with home-baked goods.

"I almost forgot!" she exclaimed, making her way to the kitchen. "Have to keep the tradition alive!"

See, kids, your great-grandmother was known for three things: God, romance, and cookies. Chocolate chip was her favorite. We had them every time I went over to visit. It wasn't unusual for her trailer to be filled with their distinct, fresh-out-of-the-oven aroma. It became for me the smell and taste of real family love. Hopefully, I've given you two the same memory I was fortunate enough to have.

"You want some?" she asked sweetly, winking at me. I quickly nodded with a smile, and she pointed to one of two chairs at her kitchen table.

In front of me, she set down a tray filled with a dozen of the biggest, softest cookies, and then sat down next to me.

I filled her in on everything that had happened: the hearing, Danielle's parents, my mother and her behavior. I also told her something else that had been weighing on my mind since the hearing was over. It was something I had not told another soul about this until that point.

"I want to do something special for Danielle before I leave, but I have no idea what to do."

Her ears perked up. If it was one thing Leona Smith knew well, it was how to give an amazing gift from the heart. She took a bite and listened intently.

"I want to get her something. Something to remember me by. I don't want her to forget about me." I hesitated, embarrassed that I had to add, "But I don't have much money."

An enormous grin spread across her face as she put her hand on mine. "You came to the right place, honey. Let's go for a ride."

A few minutes later, we were bouncing along the highway in her old Pontiac sedan, her head barely clearing the dashboard. I had no idea where we were going, but I trusted her.

I wanted to enjoy every second of our last day together, but I spent the car ride staring out the window, lost in my thoughts. I couldn't get the image of Danielle crying out of my head. Every time she cried, I had the same twist in my gut. Even though deep down I knew the idea was ridiculous, I felt as if I was the one hurting her. I focused on my reflection in the window to distract myself.

Thankfully, it wasn't long before we pulled into the vast, shadowless parking lot of the Melbourne Square Mall. Grandma left the air-conditioning running before shutting off the engine. "So, with Danielle, what's your plan after you leave?" she asked.

This was practically all I'd thought about since the hearing, and I had a plan. I was glad to have someone to confide in who wouldn't shoot it down.

I told her every detail. She listened, but her smile slowly faded as I talked, until soon she was wiping away tears. My smile had turned into the face of confusion. "What's wrong, Grandma? Do you think it won't work?"

"Honey," she said, pressing a Kleenex to the thin, sagging skin under her eyes, "you need to understand something. That is a huge thing to do for someone. Men don't do that kind of thing anymore. I'm not surprised by you, though. You always were an old soul, a real Warren Sheffield! You've told me before that you knew nothing about romance. But what you are planning to do for her after you leave is one of the most romantic things I've ever heard."

"But do you think it will work?" I pressed.

"Oh yes," she said. "What you're talking about is the type of thing women dream of! But very, very few get to live it."

She was the expert on romance, and she said that about me?

We hurried ourselves around the big mall until we found a small jewelry store near the back entrance.

I looked at her with curious eyes.

"You can't go wrong with jewelry, hon. Besides, you need something that will last. Something to really drive your point home."

My eyes widened with the glittering sparkles shining through every case of the store. I quietly tugged on her sleeve. "I don't have any money, Grandma."

She looked over at me and pretended to be shocked. "Who said you needed any?"

That was Grandma, always spoiling me. She was retired and felt it was a grandmother's right to spoil her grandchild. I squeezed her with happiness and gratitude.

An older woman behind the glass counter in the middle of the store greeted us. "Looking for something special today?"

"My grandson is getting ready to move away, and he wants to get something nice for the love of his life," she gushed. I was overwhelmed with emotion.

Finally, someone understands me! Grandma knows my feelings are real.

"I'd be so happy to help you with that. What a little romantic you are! And smart, too. Women love jewelry. I know just the thing!" She led us around another set of glass counters toward the rings. I could tell by the look on Grandma's face that that wasn't really what she was thinking of.

"I don't know about rings," she said. "We're looking for something that she won't outgrow."

We went over to watch, but that wasn't it. I wanted something perfect. I wanted something to show her how I felt about her.

My frustration was showing.

"Trust your instincts," Grandma said patiently. "You'll know it when you see it."

The jeweler was determined as well. Luckily, business was slow, so we were the only ones there to take up her full attention. She eventually led us to a case along the back wall with necklaces inside.

They were all beautiful, but they were just... jewelry, something anyone could give anyone else as an ordinary gift. This was no ordinary occasion or ordinary girl.

We looked at almost everything they had to offer. Just when I was about to give up, I saw it. The perfect gift was there at the far end of the counter, tucked in the back. I pointed at it. Grandma gasped and bounded over. She pointed, and the jeweler unlocked the case to show us.

"An excellent choice. It's the last one we have," she said, presenting the necklace. The three of us gazed at it as it hung from the jeweler's hand in the light. Small rays of light darted out from every part.

I knew nothing about jewelry, but my gut screamed that it was the right choice. It was something that would garner attention, which I knew Danielle would love. It summed up everything I felt about her and would be the perfect thing to seal the promise I was going to give her.

"This is it! This is the one! What do you think, Grandma?"

"Honey," she said, holding it up, "you're a natural romantic."

I knew Danielle was going to lose it when she saw it. My gut was never wrong. Grandma winked at me as the jeweler rang it up. Within moments, she had wrapped it in a little black box with white ribbon.

We took it and made our way out to the parking lot, fast. If Grandma was late in dropping me off, she'd be in for a tongue-lashing from Mom.

I pulled it out of the box as we pulled onto I-95. I could see my reflection in it as I held it in my hands. It was simple, yet elegant. It was beautiful, yet poignant. It was exactly what I was looking for: the perfect gift to complete the perfect gesture to the perfect girl. The girl who helped me to come out of my shell. The girl who showed me for the first time that I could be happy. The girl who made me realize that not everyone was out to hurt me, that some people were good, and some families were loving, and that I could be a part of one.

"What's wrong, hon?" Grandma asked, noticing my face forlorn.

"I have no idea what to say tomorrow. This is probably going to be one of the most important things I'll ever say to anyone!"

Grandma clicked her tongue. She reached into her glove compartment and pulled out a notepad and pen and handed it to me.

"Let's brainstorm," she said, returning her attention to the road. "Write what I tell you and practice. You get this right, and she'll never forget it."

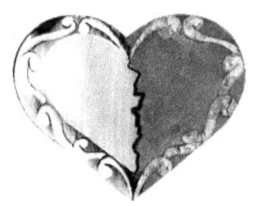

13

"I Will Always Love You"
(by Whitney Houston)

"Jesus Christ," Danielle's dad grumbled when he heard the doorbell. "It's seven a.m.!"

"It's their last day together. Just be patient," his wife said, approaching the door. She put on a happy face as she greeted me. "A little early, Chris."

"Sorry," I said as I walked over to join him at the dining room table. He had a newspaper laid out and was trying to read it. "Is Danielle here?"

"I think she's still waking up," her mom said, holding a coffee pot.

I sat at the table, gently tapping the edge as I waited. Danielle's dad looked up at me from his paper, a smirk painted on his face. His eyes fixated on my tapping hand.

"Sorry," I said, dropping my hands into my lap.

A shriek came from the hallway.

"Oh shit! Chris is here?" Danielle screamed as she bounded back into the bathroom.

"Language, Danielle!" her mom called out. She sighed and made her way over to her daughter.

"You didn't tell me Chris was here already, Mom!"

"He just got here. Don't worry about your hair!"

The door to the bathroom slammed shut, but the faint sound of hairspray and furiously detangling brush strokes broke through. Danielle's dad returned to his paper.

I watched him as he read, waiting to see if he would acknowledge the fact that this was my last day with them. Danielle's dad had always enjoyed reading the paper. It was part of his morning routine, though usually he did it around eight.

Still, part of me was hoping he would acknowledge that this was an ominous day. My deeper hope was that he might even be upset that I was leaving. But he went about his morning like it was any other day.

Catching my stare, he gave me an unamused look over the paper. Taking a deep breath, he finally spoke.

"So, today's your last day with us, eh?"

"Yes, sir."

He nodded and put the paper down on the table.

"You guys leave tomorrow?"

"Tomorrow morning, early," I replied. "Mom wants us to get on the 95 before traffic backs up."

"That's smart. Your parents are still coming here for your going-away party tonight, right? My wife has been working hard on it."

I nodded shyly. He seemed distant now, like back when I first arrived. I admit I expected some emotion, maybe even a hug or a smack on the back, something to show me he cared about me. But as the time passed that morning, I realized I wasn't going to get any of that. Not even a "We'll miss you around here, kiddo."

"I've been wanting to talk to you about something," he began sternly. "Danielle isn't good with goodbyes. She's been, well, how should I put it? *Pissy* the last few days. She's really taking your leaving hard."

I nodded again, keeping my head down.

"It's for the best. You understand that, right?"

"What do you mean?" I said, looking up at him quickly.

He cleared his throat and straightened up in the chair.

"I mean this little, whatever's happening between the two of you, it was going to end eventually. At least with your leaving the state, it won't be as messy."

What exactly is this guy getting at?

"But we aren't breaking up," I said.

He leaned in and raised his voice just a little. "Look, I get it," he started. "Saying goodbye to your first love is hard. But I can tell you from experience that it never lasts. I don't care how much you guys love each other, if you want to call it love. It never lasts."

"What would you call it?"

"Infatuation, puppy love, whatever. Not love."

"Why not?"

"You kids are too young. The two of you get to move on. She will end up with someone else, and you will end up with someone more... up your alley."

Up my alley? A lump materialized in my throat. "Is it... Do you... You still don't think I'm good enough for your daughter, do you?"

"Well, Chris, if we're being honest, no. I don't think you're good enough for my daughter."

My knuckles were turning white under the table. The nerve of this guy!

"Did she tell you I took a beating by four guys to protect her? She walked away without a single scratch on her!"

His beard reflected his hidden jaw tightening.

"Yeah, I heard," he said, unimpressed. "And I appreciate that. But I don't want her with a punching bag. And since we're speaking frankly, young man, you're swinging for the fences with her, anyway. You need to find yourself a girl in your own... league."

I couldn't believe what was happening. After all we'd been through, I'd thought he understood me. I thought he'd taken me under his wing. I felt accepted by him, like a part of the family. Why was he taking all of that away from me on my last day in his house? My chin quivered, but I fought it off.

"You're a good kid," he said, pulling back a bit. "I'm sorry for what happened with your dad. If you want my advice, learn from it. Let it make you a man. But right now, you and my daughter are a mismatch, so enjoy this for the fun day it's going to be and say goodbye when you're done. You'll find someone right for you one day."

I found someone. She's in the bathroom right now, fixing her hair. For me.

He contorted a forced smile before returning to his newspaper. I sat there, my sullen mouth ajar.

"I'm coming back," I suddenly spoke, snapping out of my daze of dejection.

He didn't even take his eyes off his newspaper.

"Oh yeah? When?"

"I don't know yet."

He flapped the newspapers in his hands.

My nostrils flared and my head felt fuzzy. The only other person who'd ever made me feel this way was my father. I wanted to leap across the table and shake some sense into him. Just as I was about to open my mouth again, a soft voice caught my attention.

"Hey." Danielle stood at the mouth of the hallway, smiling at me. She wore the same fuzzy pink robe she wore that first day when I caught her spying on us. Her hair was straight now that she had combed it. The emerald in her eyes was shining more than usual.

She held out her hand, and I jumped to take it as she kissed me on the lips. Danielle's dad rolled his eyes as he watched us disappear down the hall toward her room.

"Door open, Danielle," he commanded. She rolled her eyes as we ventured down the hall.

"You're early," she said as she shut the door behind us.

"I couldn't sleep last night. I want to spend as much time with you as I can."

She laughed, crinkling her eyes. She gently pushed me down onto her pink and purple bed and nestled in, placing her head on my chest.

We lay like that for a while, quietly just enjoying the feeling of being together.

"I don't want you to go," she said softly.

The knife that had been plunged into my heart by my father days earlier was now twisting. I carefully wiped away a tear. I hated this day already.

Suddenly, she jerked upright. "What are you thinking about right now?" she asked. Without saying a word, I sat up and pulled the small velvet box from my jeans pocket. Now was the perfect time.

"What is this?" she asked, smiling devilishly.

"This is for you."

Her smile grew as she opened the box. The sterling silver inside glistened in the light coming from her bedside lamp.

She let out a small gasp, her hand coming up to her mouth. "I love it!"

Delicately, I lifted from the box a heart pendant edged with filigree, and pinched both of its thin chains, dangling it in front of us.

"I was up all-night practicing what I'm about to say," I said, drawing in a deep breath.

She fixed her eyes on mine reverently. Even though I had known her for three years, my hands still shook as I pushed forward.

"This is my heart." I said, gently snapping the pendant in half as it was designed to do. The act revealed a zigzag on each piece where the two halves met.

"It's broken because I have to leave you and I don't want to."

She held her hand up to her mouth as her eyes watered. I put one half on the bed and focused on the other. Unclasping the chain, I moved her hair to expose her neck like I'd seen men do in TV commercials for jewelry. A moment later, we were both captivated by the sight of the half heart resting between the lapels of her fuzzy bathrobe.

"This half is yours," I continued. "When you see it, remember that I will love you for the rest of my life."

She let out a small snort as the tears journeyed down her cheeks.

I picked up the other half from the bed.

"Wait," she said, wiping her eyes with her sleeve. She took it from my hands and motioned for me to turn around. With slow movement, she clasped the second half around my neck as I had done with her. "What is this half for?" she asked, her voice shaking.

"This half is to remind me I am not complete until I come back to you. You really should have the whole thing because you have had my heart since the day I met you."

"You mean you're going to come back?"

"I promise. Because I will always love you."

Her face was completely red as she hugged me, her shoulders shuddering, her cries loud and wet. I accepted her, holding her, holding myself together, so we didn't become one big mess of tears. It felt as if everything she had been holding in for weeks now came out all at once. I had to be strong enough to support her.

"This will always be your home," she said, sobbing. "And I will always love you. I will always love you, Chris. I will always love you."

We sat on the edge of her bed and embraced until we were all cried out.

"You came up with all that yourself?" she asked, wiping her eyes.

"Well, not exactly," I said sheepishly. "My grandma helped me a little."

She laughed as she wiped her eyes with a tissue.

"I like your grandmother," she said. "I wish I could have met her."

"Me, too. But she knows all about you. She thinks we're perfect for each other, and that she says that young love is the purest. And she loves you, too. She's loved you for a long time."

We looked into each other's eyes as each moment passed. We both knew this was going to be our last time together. To pull herself together, Danielle took a deep breath and went to the bathroom to wash her face. "We need to get ready," she called back to me. "Let's make the most we can out of today."

I smiled and looked out her door, which had magically opened on its own. I saw her dad's shadow looming at the head of the table. He had moved to the opposite end closest to our door, no doubt eavesdropping.

I may be gone, but I'm still going to be around.

• •

Around sunset, my mom and Dick arrived with chips and dip for my party.

Danielle and I eventually entered, holding hands. It felt like our new jewelry was lit up in neon, the way the adults stared at us.

Danielle's dad frowned as his wife gasped.

"Oh my goodness, how beautiful, Danielle!"

Danielle looked down at her pendant and blushed.

"And I see you've got one as well, Chris. Oh! Two halves of a single heart, right? How romantic."

"Yeah, a single heart," I answered proudly.

She walked up to us warmly and inspected the necklaces. "Is this your going away present to Danielle?"

I nodded. She looked at me with approval. *Take that!*

"It's good to see that some men still know what romance is. You're going to make some lucky girl very happy one day."

Danielle and I looked at each other. *Why are adults so dense?*

He grumbled under his breath.

"I just can't get over how much you've grown in the last three years, Chris," her mom went on, hugging us both.

"Inspiration helps," I said, kissing Danielle on the head. She smiled and hugged me tighter.

"All right!" her dad barked. "Let's get this thing going. These guys can't stay too late. They're leaving early tomorrow morning for Michigan!"

The adults set up the card table in the dining room. Danielle and I set up a blanket in front of the television in the adjacent living room. We cuddled up on the floor, our backs against the couch. Flipping through the channels, we settled on one of her favorite movies, *Willy Wonka and the Chocolate Factory.*

My attention was less on the Oompa-Loompas than it was on Danielle. She never stopped fiddling with her pendant, turning it in her fingers. Somewhere between the snozzberry wallpaper and Violet blowing up like a blueberry, Danielle nuzzled even closer into my side and held both halves of our heart in her hand. She tried to be discreet, but I could feel her pressing tears into our clothes.

Her tears finally subsided as she got into the movie. She softly sang along with "Pure Imagination" and I closed my eyes to seal her voice into my memory forever.

All the other kids were gone now. Only Charlie and his grandpa remained when I realized Danielle was struggling to stay awake. "You okay?" I said, giving her a little shake.

"I'm good... I'm up... just sleepy. I don't wanna sleep though. I'm gonna be awake when you leave." She gave me a glassy-eyed smile.

"It's okay," I said, kissing her forehead. Her eyes closed against her will, but mine stayed wide open, trying to memorize the curve of her chin, the color of her cheeks, the freckles under her eyes, her cute button nose, where her bangs fell, just shy of her eyes. I stared at her until I was sure I'd committed every detail to my mind. Then, closing my eyes, I breathed in the smell of her strawberry shampoo.

I glanced over at the adults, who were laughing and yelling, happy with their lives. The step that separated the dining room from the living room divided two completely different worlds. They were adults, free to do as they wanted, and we were not. Tonight, I held onto the only person who ever truly loved me, and tomorrow they would separate us without a second thought. I began to softly sob, taking care not to wake her.

STOP.

The voice came as a jolt, clapping through my mind like thunder. Dutifully, I did as I was told, though I did not know whose command I was following.

Take control of your life.

They think they have everything figured out about you. Dick, he can't stand you. He thinks you're a moron. Mom? Everything she thinks about you is all wrong. Danielle's mom? She's been nice to you, but she doesn't see you as a man any more than her dad does. Her dad was right. Getting the crap beaten out of you doesn't make you good enough for Danielle.

I glanced over at the group of them, oblivious to their own cruelty, then down at the angel slumbering in my arms.

That's right. You love her. It courses through your veins. The two of you have a bond that they will never understand. They don't know your future, and they don't know shit about the power of love.

Take control, it continued. *You determine your future, not them. Go to Michigan, become the man she knows you are, and come back for her.*

Leave weak little C.J. in the past where he belongs. You are no longer that person. You don't need a father, or someone like her father. He will see in time how wrong he was about you, and he will apologize. You know what you need to do. Just do it. Prove everyone else wrong and become the man she deserves.

The voice in my head had never been so vocal before, but it showed up at the right time with this pep talk.

"I'll prove to you how much I love you," I whispered, kissing Danielle again. She shifted a little, repositioning herself closer to me.

"I love you, too," she whispered faintly before drifting off again.

In that tender moment, something inside me snapped. I felt a mental dislodging from the person I used to be, as if a part had broken off and was now independent from its host.

A new person seemed to emerge from this foreign part within my psyche, someone with an energy I had never felt before. It felt unrelenting and unstoppable. The love I felt for this girl seemed to fill me with an intense determination I had never felt before. The pain I felt in those moments only seemed to intensify the energy this person exuded.

One thing was for sure: this person was not C.J.

I continued to hold her until Mom and Dick called over that it was time to go. I didn't wake Danielle because I knew neither of us could handle any more goodbyes. As I looked at her for the last time, I already started planning exactly what I would say when I saw her again. I would tell her the story of how I fell in love with the girl next door, remained faithful to her for years, and returned with one simple request: give us another chance.

And with that, the happiest chapter of my childhood was done.

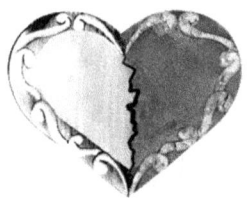

14

"This Used to Be My Playground"
(by Madonna)

A wave of tension washed over me as my mother rushed past. "Hurry and grab a box," she belted out. "We're running behind schedule!" Moving boxes stacked four high lined the entire length of our hallway.

She grabbed two and rushed back past me again, huffing and disappearing out of the front door. We were always running behind schedule.

Dick came by next, copying the same behavior: yelling at me, grabbing boxes, and rushing outside. "Move your ass and make yourself useful for once!" He tripped over the step leading to the front door. I chuckled rather loudly, something I had never done before for fear of getting into trouble.

When I woke up that morning, I felt like a different person. I was no longer afraid of getting into trouble. I didn't care. I didn't care if Dick or anyone got mad at me anymore. Even if he threatened to hit me, I didn't care. From this point on, I cared about one thing only: getting back to Danielle.

Mom appeared again and shot me a look. "Christopher James, move your butt right now!"

I picked up a box. I may not have cared about Dick getting mad, but my mother was a different story altogether. He made threats of punishment, whereas she made promises and followed through. Even this new version of me knew his limits.

As we continued carrying boxes to the moving van, I looked across the street with each pass, hoping for a glimpse of Danielle spying on us. But her house showed no signs of life. Even the kitchen light was out, a telltale sign her dad was reading his paper. I wondered if she was still sleeping in the same spot on the floor when we left last night or if her parents had transferred her to her bed.

"Out of the way, lazy fuck!" Dick shoved me out of my reverie as he carried the last of the boxes out. He was usually more careful not to cuss at me when Mom was nearby. She had caught him one time calling me an asshole, which lead to a divorce threat if it ever happened again.

I carried the last box into the van, Mom locking the front door behind us as we exited. "Time to go," she said, flustered. Dick was already in the moving van and pulling out of the driveway. I dragged my feet behind Mom toward our Ford Aerostar, my eyes still glued to Danielle's house.

Time slowed as I hung on every second with hope for a last glimpse. The engine started. My seatbelt clicked. *This shouldn't be happening.*

My eyes drooped in my blank face as my memory painted the empty world outside. I saw Danielle standing on our sidewalk in her bathrobe on the first day I saw her. I looked over at her front door and saw the neighborhood kids getting chased out because they dared speak ill of the boy she loved. I saw myself knocking on that door day after day after day.

The Aerostar slowly moved forward, as if my mother was reminiscing as well. The pavement crunched under the tires from the weight of the van. I took a last look at the tire swing where we had our first kiss, now motionless and empty. I saw myself pushing Danielle, her feet dangling, her giddy screams echoing.

I was determined to keep my eyes locked on her house, a last, futile effort to not let her go. I refused to relent, even when the house was the size of a pea. The house I lived in for three years didn't even exist.

At the intersection of Fairhaven and Crocus, I could see the bus pulling up for our first day of school. I remembered how nervous I was when that beautiful girl smiled at me, when she took me by the hand.

"You're with me!" her voice said, echoing in my memory. I snapped back to reality long enough to wipe the tears from my face before they leapt from my chin.

I always will be with you.

But eventually, all those meaningful places vanished into the distance as the neighborhood blurred into the I-95 and we left the neighborhood.

Blankly, I stared out the passenger window as we continued north. I didn't care where we were anymore. I didn't care where we were going. It didn't matter to me how great our life was supposed to be now that my father was gone. Their life was going to be great, not mine.

And yet I felt different, like a butterfly who had been struggling to emerge from his cocoon now feeling the vastness of the world all around. For the first time in my life, I was awake, finally aware of my potential. Somehow, I knew this was truly a new beginning for me.

Sitting there, my mind focused on the world passing by, driving away from the only life I'd ever experienced happiness in, I wasn't despondent like I thought I would be. I wasn't tearing myself down or feeling sorry for myself. I wasn't that sad child anymore. I felt the same energy I had from the night before, only it was stronger and more prevalent, as if what I had been before was turning into an empty husk.

With that energy arose a red-hot fury at the powerlessness that had come from my previous condition. It disgusted me the way I had allowed myself to be pushed around, told what to feel, to think, who to love.

That changes when we cross the state line, I thought as we approached Georgia.

Like a butterfly, I would emerge from my old self completely transformed. I would cast aside that weak and brittle husk that I had worn since my birth and grow armor in its place. At thirteen, I could feel my body developing into that of a man, and I resolved to develop that body to reflect my new personality. This was no longer the body of a boy. This was now the body of a man in charge of his own life, a man able to make his own decisions, a man able to protect himself *and* the people he loved.

The husk of C.J. would soon be gone.

Change had begun, and when the time was right, I would return to the one person I loved. I didn't just make a promise to Danielle. It was a promise I made to myself. My father was wrong. I didn't need him. I'd be my own father if I had to. And I would earn Danielle's father's respect. And in the end, I would earn his daughter's hand, finally free to live a life with her that previous generations of my family never knew.

When a man knows the love of an amazing woman, he will cross any mountain to win her back. If he can't go over it, he will go through it. If he can't go through it, he will move it. My mountain wasn't my parents. It wasn't Danielle's parents, either. It was me. It was my family's past. The abuse had to end, and it would end with me. I would succeed where three other generations of my family had failed. I would do it for the love of my life, the one person who ever truly loved me. One day, I would tell her all about it.

As we crossed the state line, I opened the window and threw my hand into the sky, tossing the husk of my former self to the side of the road, leaving it to rot with the past. A new future had begun. And until I returned, a countdown would begin.

A man who is determined alone is persistent, but a man who combines that determination with intelligence is inevitable.

I love you, Danielle.

2,699 days remaining...

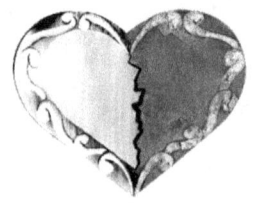

15

"Waking Light"
(by Beck)

We arrived in Grayling, Michigan after two days on the road. Grayling was a small, podunk town in northern Michigan, its only claim to fame a nearby Army base.

But my mother's aunt lived there with her two sons, so we had a place to land. With winter approaching, we learned quickly that temperatures in our new state dipped below freezing frequently. It wasn't unusual to be stranded indoors for days after a storm.

We lived with my mother's aunt for around four months. Her house was a dainty shack, a blip on the twenty-mile woodland map outside town. The entire time we lived there, I slept on a two-cushion couch in the living room that had a hard spot in the middle. That and the fact that I awoke often to find my great aunt staring at me made things even more uncomfortable. I don't recall getting a single full night's rest the entire time we were there.

Being trapped indoors by a blizzard with an intrusive, bossy, bipolar aunt caused the newfound chip on my shoulder to grow into a boulder. My patience and my propensity to mind my mouth were both wavering at an alarming rate. With no friends, nothing to do, and a great resentment for being where I was, I was a ticking time bomb.

Four months into our stay, our inevitable clash came to pass after she jumped on me for taking too long in the shower. She stood in front of me, waving her fat finger and going off on another one of her illogical tirades.

"I'm sick and tired of you not helping around here. You expect me to feed you and keep a roof over your head without having to do anything to earn it?"

"I try to help. I've tried to help on more than one occasion, remember?" I shot back. "You told me each time that I was your guest and that I didn't have to help!"

"You little..." she growled, lifting her hand up. Then, thinking better of it, she lowered her hand and left.

Her gravelly voice continued as she shifted a curtain to look out the window. "Perfect. Snow stopped. You go outside to the picnic bench there and sit until I give you permission to get up!"

I glared at her. *You're going to discipline me?*

"There's like four inches of snow out there!"

"Then you better clear it off first." she said, folding her arms in front of her.

"It's below freezing!"

"Bundle up."

I wanted to smack her. Even though I would come to know the impulse for violence more and more, I swore to myself I would never act on it. I grabbed my coat and gloves and marched outside. I knew my parents would hit the roof once they returned from town. When we arrived in Grayling, my great aunt had agreed with my parents that they were the only ones who would discipline me.

I cleared enough of the powder off to sit and curled into a small ball, my dreams of better times keeping me warm.

I was right. When Mom and Dick found me outside, they got into a nasty fight with her. This incident was enough to start our departure from her home.

Our new house downtown was smaller than my great aunt's place, but I finally had some privacy. Originally, I thought being downtown would allow me access to more people so I could make friends, but I was still having difficulty fitting in. That all changed one day at school.

I entered eighth grade at Southwest Middle School like a fish walking on land. One advantage of moving to a new state is that you can start over completely clean. No one knew anything about me. No one had ever heard of C.J. Since they held me back in pre-kindergarten, I was older than most of the kids and stuck out like a sore thumb.

I sat at lunch by myself, as I'd grown accustomed to doing. This continued until one day when a kid randomly approached me. Like me, he wore glasses and had dark brown hair, though he was better managed. Unlike me, he was the most popular kid at our small school. To my surprise, he sat at my table and smiled.

"You must be new here," he said. "I'm Ryan."

People just come out of the blue and talk to you here?

He held out his hand, and I reluctantly accepted it. I suddenly noticed that I wasn't cowering anymore. My shoulders were back, and I held my head high. I looked him right in the eyes. My new beginning had already begun.

"I'm Chris."

"Hi, Chris," he said. Pointing a finger at a small group of boys at a table nearby.

"You wanna come sit with us?"

I couldn't resist the smile on my face. I was making friends. After taking him up on his offer, I headed over with my paper bag lunch. The boys he had pointed out earlier gave him a puzzled look as I sat down. They each introduced themselves: Steve, Joey, Mark, and Justin.

Upon arriving, I picked up on an awkward vibe; they seemed a little hesitant about accepting me into the fold. I kept quiet without being too timid, just listening and observing as they went on about mundane topics.

After that first day, Ryan treated me like I was just one of the guys. Every day, the six of us would meet and eat our lunches together at the biggest table in the cafeteria. We were the center of attention. While I was still uncomfortable with the idea of being looked at as people walked by, I very much enjoyed not being alone all the time.

The boys didn't seem too interested in me. Ryan would try to include me in the group, asking me questions about where I came from and what my family was like. After a week, curiosity must have gotten the better of the group because Joey suddenly plopped down and began interviewing me.

"I've been meaning to ask you something. What's the deal with your necklace?"

Even though I wasn't quite comfortable with them just yet, I couldn't help myself. "It's for a girl I have back home."

"A girl?" Steve chimed in. "You have a girlfriend? Why did you leave her to come here, of all places?"

I shrugged. "Came here with my parents."

The guys looked around at each other, shrugged, and lost interest again. Within moments, they were back to talking about the girls and mundane topics. But Ryan kept his eye on me, like he knew I wasn't telling them everything.

That day he invited me to the bowling alley, the usual spot where he waited for his mom to pick him up after school. The two of us sat in a booth in front of an empty lane and shared some cheese sticks.

"So, what's the deal with your necklace, really?" he asked.

"What do you mean?"

"You can tell me the truth. Is there really a girl back where you came from?"

"Yes!" I snapped defensively. "Her name is Danielle."

He looked at me inquisitively. "Why did your parents want to move here?"

I found myself in uncharted territory. I barely knew this guy, but I felt comfortable with him. I wasn't sure if it was his pleasant nature that opened me up, that he was so accepting of me, or my commitment to be confident in this new phase of my life, but that day I let go and told him everything.

I told him all about Danielle, about my parents' divorce, including the hearing. I unloaded about my frustration with how my family treated me and even the conclusion with my father. He listened intently as I spilled my guts. I was surprised by how good it felt to finally talk about all this with someone other than Danielle.

"I know what you mean," he said at last. I could only give him a confused look.

How do you know what I mean? Your life is perfect! You come from a wealthy family. You're good-looking, with your gelled-back hair and square jaw. You're popular. Everyone knows you. All the girls talk to you. You're the center of attention all the time! You don't know what I mean!

"My parents are in the middle of a divorce right now. They're getting ready to go to court to complete everything, I guess," he said. "The worst part is, like you said, they used me to get back at each other, making me report about what the other says and does."

I took a sip of my Coke. *So what? Lots of parents divorce. That's nothing like what I just confessed.*

Then the floodgates opened.

"I know what you're thinking. Everyone thinks my life is perfect, but it's not. No one listens to me at home. No one cares what I think or how I feel about all this shit going on," he pulled apart the paper napkins on the table. "My dad is a drunk who works all the time. When he's not working, he's passed out — I mean, when he's not smacking me and my brother around. I know there's a chance, like, he could get custody of me, and if he does, I don't know what I'll do. All my parents care about is hurting each other, and they pull me into the middle of it like I'm nothing. No one cares that our family is being torn apart or all the shitty things that could happen next. I just feel like I have nowhere to go and no one to talk to."

Wow. It's like looking in a mirror.

"God, it felt good to say that," he added with a sigh. "Thanks for opening up to me, man."

I reached out and grabbed a cheese stick. In a poised, dignified way, I shoved it in my mouth. Maybe that's the first thing I needed to do to change for Danielle: listen more, be a shoulder to lean on. "I'll listen if you want to talk," I said with my mouth full.

He looked up at me, a small smile spreading across his face. He took his soda can and held it up as a toast. I returned the sentiment and the two of us brought them together.

"Friends?" he asked as we held the cans together.

I smiled, a large crumb sticking out from the side of my mouth. "Friends."

We both chugged our sodas in unison.

"So, what are you going to do about Danielle?" he asked, shifting his focus back to the pendant.

I looked down at it, admiring it for a moment.

"I'm going to get her back someday. She got me through everything. She's my best friend."

He seemed sullen again as he stared at it. "I've never had a girlfriend before," he said. "I wish I had someone like that."

I looked at him in disbelief. He was the most popular kid in school. All the girls seemed to like him. Someone like *him* was jealous of *me*? Did we cross into the twilight zone on the way up here?

"You will," I said. "Just give it time. I wish I could be popular like you."

His mouth turned down in disgust. "Why? None of those people are my friends. They only pretend to be my friend because of what I do for them. By being with me, they're popular! If I lost my status, they'd want nothing to do with me."

"They seem okay to me."

"You don't know them like I do. They're absorbed in their own little world, completely oblivious to others around them. If that's normal, I hate it. You're lucky. You have someone who loves you for who you are. She's going to love you no matter what. Never let that go."

I smiled at the thought. He was right. We ordered another plate of sticks. As we destroyed that greasy food like only teenage boys can do, I realized things were turning around. Maybe there was hope after all.

• •

At school, things seemed to improve after Ryan and I officially became friends. For the next few months, I enjoyed going to school. My attitude cooled off. Even my parents remarked that I seemed happier, my mom hinting, "I told you so."

Being friends with a popular kid had its perks. For starters, no one picked on me. We sat at the best lunch table in the school. With everyone else, he was jovial and a natural at being the center of attention. All the girls talked to him. (They ignored me, but I didn't care.)

Then after school, Ryan and I would hang out at the bowling alley, just us, playing games. If we were bored, we'd do our homework. With me, he was more relaxed than he was with everyone else. He seemed to take life slower and wasn't as eager to please.

From the way he spoke to me, it seemed as if he didn't have to impress me. One time, he told me he loved hanging out with me because, for the first time, he felt he could just be himself. I could feel that our friendship was as helpful to him as it was to me. Having him around helped me get my mind off missing Danielle. Hanging out with me got his mind off what was going in his life as well.

But despite saying he felt comfortable, he didn't talk much more about his parents' divorce in progress. This changed around the holidays. As they moved toward the hearing, he told me he was in the same predicament I was once in. He seemed depressed but tried to play it off.

Things worsened for him as we went into December. The judge granted his father sole custody of both Ryan and his brother. Ryan was near tears when he told us all at lunch that his dad was forcing them to move to Wisconsin the following month. I wondered if what I felt then was how Danielle felt.

When we said goodbye on the last day before Christmas break, he hugged me. "Thank you for being such a good friend. I'm really going to miss you," he said into my ear.

"Yeah dude, me too," I said, a little confused by the depth of his emotion. "I'll see you after break."

The holidays came and went uneventfully. But when school started up again, I didn't see Ryan anywhere. I found the guys and asked if any of them had heard from him. They seemed quieter than usual. Mark looked up at me and said blankly, "You didn't hear?"

I leaned in toward him. "Hear what?"

They looked at each other; the vibe shifting uncomfortably in seconds.

"Ryan killed himself two days ago," Justin said. "Went out to the woods next to his house and put his dad's twelve-gauge in his mouth."

I had to catch myself from falling. I couldn't breathe.

"The funeral is Saturday," Steve added blankly.

I just sat there, staring out into space.

Joey cleared his throat. "You guys were close, huh?"

Close? He was my best friend! I focused my eyes on him, still too shocked to respond.

"Sorry," he huffed. "We didn't know if like... We thought maybe he had you around because he felt sorry for you."

"What?" I growled.

"I said sorry! We just assumed because, you know, how you are and everything."

The disgust I felt for all of them was overwhelming. Ryan was right about them. They were horrible! I stood up and walked away. I went to the school nurse and said I was sick. My mother eventually came and picked me up. I didn't say a word on the ride home.

I said nothing until the next afternoon.

• •

The funeral was a packed church. My parents dropped me off, Dick telling me I had to face this on my own. The entire school showed up, even the staff. Teachers were crying and hugging each other as soft organ music played in the background.

I went up to his open coffin, which was situated just to the left of a podium. Ryan lay there, his hands clasped together in his lap. He looked horrible. His skin was pale, much more than when he was alive. It seemed to have a waxy texture to it. The back of his head was concealed well and was pressed into a deep pillow.

It was my first time experiencing death. The iciness of his hand shocked me as I touched him.

I kneeled before the casket when it was my turn and pretended to pray like everyone else. All I could do was pretend because I didn't have any prayers to say. I just looked at him, replaying in my mind his last words to me. *Thanks for being such a good friend.*

He already knew what he was going to do. He had planned it and was saying goodbye. I just didn't realize it when he said it to me.

I went up to the guys, who were seated two rows back. There was just enough room for one more in their row. I motioned to sit down, and Mark stopped me. "Oh, hey. We're saving this for someone. Sorry."

And just like that, I was cast aside. I was no longer welcome, no longer "one of the guys." I turned to look at Ryan and then back at them. They were laughing amongst themselves. All the other seats were full, with only standing room in the very back.

The sea of mourners blocked the view of the casket from the back. I observed the guys as they laughed and carried on like this funeral was at the school cafeteria. Some teachers scolded them, but they started back up again as soon as they were away.

Listening to the service, my attention drifted to my own thoughts. *All he wanted was for someone to accept him for who he really was. I guess he had me, sure, but had I done enough for him? Could I have stopped this?* He was the only friend I'd ever had besides Danielle, and he killed himself.

Then, of course, I thought about Danielle. *Ryan said he was jealous of me, that he wished he had someone like her. If I didn't have Danielle, would I have killed myself, too? Why was I so lucky and he wasn't?* A sense of self-pity washed over me. I was crying, both for Ryan and for myself. I suddenly felt the temptation to start self-loathing again.

I found myself touching the pendant hung around my neck. Its cold, smooth surface seemed to comfort me. I rubbed my finger over the jagged edge where the heart broke. Closing my eyes, I could smell the strawberries again. For a few moments, we were together again. But something else was in my head as well. That familiar voice from Danielle's house shot itself back into my brain.

Quit feeling sorry for yourself! Danielle's man doesn't sulk. He doesn't feel sorry for himself! He gets up, and he keeps moving forward into what's waiting for him. Ryan would want you to go get her back. Be the man who does it. Straighten up! Is this how you would want her dad to see you?

The voice was right. The temptation toward regression, toward weakness and self-loathing, went up in smoke. *So, you're going to be alone, so what? They rejected you. Who cares? You're not alone. Someone loves you, and one day you're going back to her. You must overcome this shit first, though. Be the man who deserves her!*

These would become my thoughts each morning as I looked in the mirror, before pulling my shirt down over the pendant that rested there on my heart. *All of this is a test to strengthen me because I have a destiny to fulfill.*

I took a deep breath, dried my tears, straightened up, and left the church. Ryan would understand.

I went back to eating lunch by myself. This time, I was truly okay with it. Through Ryan, I had seen both sides of being popular and realized what was truly important: those who accept you for who you are unconditionally. I also realized how hard those people were to find, even if you were charming and good-looking. It only made me cherish Danielle more.

Then one evening, three months after Ryan's funeral, I came home to see my mother in tears.

"My mom passed away last night. The three of us are going down to Coldwater for her service."

I barely knew my mom's mom, so I didn't have much of a reaction. "When are we coming back?" I asked.

Mom took a deep breath, trying to compose herself.

"We're not. Pack your things."

2,250 days remaining...

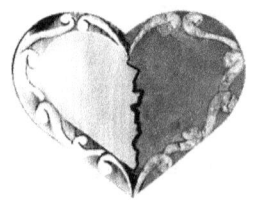

16

"Tonight, Tonight"
(by The Smashing Pumpkins)

When we arrived in Coldwater, we went straight to the hospital where they were preparing to transport the grandmother I'd never met to a funeral home. My mother wanted to see her one last time before she was cremated.

Dick and I waited by the ambulance entrance, Dick puffing furiously on a cigarette. He was even more disgruntled than usual, pissed about the decision to leave Grayling for Coldwater, an opinion he made abundantly clear on the drive down. His incessant bickering had pushed my mother to where she snapped at him to shut up.

Yet there we stood as the sun disappeared behind the trees. The snow had vanished, and the wildlife was reemerging from winter's slumber. Neither one of us said a word as the crickets ushered in the evening.

I was thinking about Ryan. Even though we were only friends for a short time, his friendship meant a lot to me. I was still processing everything that had happened.

My sullen self-reflection was short-lived as a crowd of extended family suddenly appeared around us. One by one, I was introduced to people who I had only heard about through stories. I did my best to be polite, but I was uncomfortable around so many strangers.

Among the crowd were the Hydes. They were local to Coldwater, living nearby, where we'd soon end up. There was Bonnie, my mother's sister, and her husband Bob. They had five children: Patrick, Lee, Michael, Katie, and Vicky

Lee and Michael were the only ones there at the hospital that day. Lee was fifteen years older than me, but Michael and I were only two years apart, so we connected more as we talked.

Aunt Bonnie was welcoming, in a normal way, but Bob freaked me out. He was friendly, but he kept staring at me intensely. His eyes looked small behind aviator-rimmed glasses, just south of a large red baseball cap with a picture of a deer and the silhouette of a woman's naked rear. Under the figures, it read, "I hunt white tail all year round."

His face was round with pronounced cheeks. His shoulders were broad, and he had the classic style of a country boy: blue jeans and a red checkered button up.

What is this guy's deal?

• •

Two days later marked the second funeral I'd ever attended. The service was quaint, with few attendees, after which we went to the Hyde house for the wake.

Their family home was small, a two-story house nestled amongst the suburbs. Within moments of our arrival, its walls were shaking with the sounds of laughter, commotion and Garth Brooks. Mom and Aunt Bonnie sat on the living room couch and shared stories about their mother while Dick floated around, mingling.

Michael and I really got to know each other when I learned he had a Nintendo in his room downstairs in the basement. We talked while playing the Legend of Zelda and munching on hors d'oeuvres we'd snuck down.

He was preparing for his last year of middle school, which put him a grade behind me. I liked that we had the same taste in video games, but what really impressed me was that he took karate lessons on Tuesdays.

"That's cool. You're lucky," I said as he shoved another mouthful of pizza bites in his mouth.

"What do you mean?"

"Your parents let you take karate. I've been wanting to do that for a long time."

He paused the game and looked sideways at me through his thick glasses. "What's stopping you?"

"My mom," I said, staring at the paused screen. "She hates fighting and tells me to avoid it, no matter what."

Michael scoffed and shook his head. "You can't do that. Doesn't she realize you're becoming a freshman this year? You'll be a target for sure."

He was right. Being the new kid attracted a lot of attention, mostly bad in my experience. My mother didn't care because she knew my past problems with bullies and still held on to the whole "they're doing it because they want to be friends and don't know how to ask" theory. It's always easy not to care when you're not the one affected.

"That sucks," my cousin said. "My dad isn't that way at all. He pushed me to get into karate. I can't wait to be a black belt."

"Black belt? What does that mean?"

His eyebrows raised at my ignorance. "Black belt means you are good at it. My dad is a black belt. Your dad was, too."

Everything came screeching to a halt.

"You know my dad?"

He laughed at the confused look on my face. "Yeah, we all do. Well, I've never actually met him, but my dad has told me all about him. He sounds awesome."

What?

Michael's bemused look suddenly shifted to concern. "Go ask my dad. He'll tell you. And grab a Coke while you're up there."

Great. So now everyone knows my dad? Am I having a nightmare? "He sounds awesome?" How much do they know about me?

Walking back up to the main floor, I tried desperately to make sense of what was happening. How did my dad convince everyone here that he was a great guy?

Am I ever going to leave my past behind? I swear to God if they call me C.J....

I approached the cooler and saw Bob standing nearby. I gave him a polite smile. He waved his hand, inviting me over. Reluctantly, I went, a Coke in each hand.

"How you holding up?" he asked, slapping me on the shoulder. I cringed a little as he made contact. He appeared taken aback by my reaction, but said nothing.

"I'm good."

He smiled and took a step back, looking me up and down.

Okay. Now this is really making me uncomfortable.

He shook his head as he leaned against a nearby table.

"Sorry if I'm creeping you out, Christopher. I just can't get over how much you look like him!"

Here we go.

"Your dad!" he said, laughing. "You're a spitting image of him. I had to do a double take last night."

"You know my dad?" I asked, trying to sound surprised.

"Yeah! We were best friends growing up. We even served in Korea when we were both in the Army."

Best friends, huh? So, did he become the way he was because of you, or despite you?

"How's he doing?" Bob asked.

"I don't know," I answered. "He hasn't spoken to me in over a year."

The reminiscent of happiness dropped from Bob's face.

"Why?"

I debated my next words carefully. I didn't want to shy away from the truth or dance around it awkwardly. If they were expecting C.J., some little kid they could push around, they were about to have a rude awakening.

"I wouldn't lie for him in court," I said sharply, looking him in the eye. I looked off into the other room, showing how little I cared about his reaction. "At least that's what he seemed most pissed about when he disowned me."

"Your dad disowned you?"

"Yep. That's my dad," I said, looking back at him with contempt.

Bob looked as if I had just told him he had four hours left to live. "That's... that's not the man I knew. The man I knew wouldn't do such a thing."

Even more brash now, I pressed him. "Would the 'man' you knew almost beat his wife to death in front of his kids? Would he whip his sons with a belt? What about cheating on his wife? Would he do that too?"

The color drained from Bob's face. He clumsily reached behind to find a seat and plopped into it, staring out into the abyss.

"Looks like we know two different versions of the same person."

Bob moved his hand over his face as if trying to wake up. His eyes then shifted back to me, as if coming to from a trance. He looked like he was about to say something, but I beat him to the punch. "I have to go. Michael is waiting for his soda."

"Yeah. All right."

"Kathi!" he called out as I left. "Can you come in here, please?"

Mom joined him at the table. I stopped in the doorway to the basement and watched them as they talked. Bob was almost in tears. Then he turned and gave me a look that I will never forget. It was the look of a man who was suddenly faced with a truth that broke his heart.

To this day, I don't know why he did it, but he would soon step in where his former best friend fell short. He would come to play a major role in preparing me for my return to Danielle. In the end, he would prove to be the greatest man I've ever known.

2,248 days remaining...

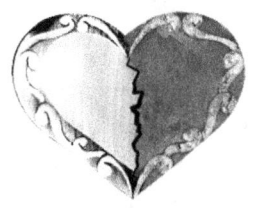

17

"Quasimodo"
(by Lifehouse)

The doorbell rang early on the day we moved into a two-bedroom rental on Chicago Street, near the center of Coldwater. Dick opened the door.

"It's Bob and Lee," he called out to my mother, sounding irritated.

"Sorry to bother you guys," Bob said, "but we thought we'd come help. I heard you still have some heavy furniture in the truck."

"I can handle it," Dick muttered.

"Nah, it's okay. No sense in hurting yourself, right? We'll get it done quicker, too. Plus, we wanted to invite you guys over for a welcome-to-the-neighborhood barbecue at our place later."

After conferring with Mom, Dick reluctantly agreed. He hated accepting help from others, as he believed it made him look weak. He opened the door to allow them in, narrowing his eyes at me as he walked by.

"Hey, Christopher!" Bob said as he entered. He seemed to always have a big grin when he saw me.

"Hey," I replied politely.

Each time he visited, Bob would make it a point to talk to me about anything and everything. He talked about his life—he was an avid hunter who enjoyed barbecuing his prizes—and asked me about mine.

Although he seemed genuine, I remained suspicious of this man, my father's self-proclaimed best friend.

It didn't take very long to get the dressers and washer/dryer moved in with all four of us men tackling it. Dick was always the first to touch each item and bark out instructions on how it should be moved. Bob and Lee took it in stride.

We took them up on their barbecue invitation, and before long, I was mingling with Bob again. He was so welcoming to me, which felt strange since I had been rather standoffish since we arrived. The more time I spent with him, the less he seemed like my dad. Still, I monitored him. When we left, he emphasized I was welcome back anytime.

I took him up on his offer and began hanging out more often with Michael. It was better than being at home, waiting for the next argument between Mom and Dick. At least there I wasn't holed up in a room with nothing but headphones and a Walkman.

Michael and I continued to bond over video games and soon became good friends. I began staying overnight and grew accustomed to waking up to the heavenly smell of homemade biscuits and gravy the next morning.

"This is why I love Sundays!" Michael proclaimed as he ran up to the kitchen, almost tripping on the stairs. I went into the living room to wait for him to finish.

"Christopher, aren't you going to eat?" Bob said, sticking his head out of the kitchen.

"I don't want to impose."

"Bullshit!" he shouted; it was his favorite phrase. He always said it with such conviction, heightening his voice on the "shit" part. I eventually borrowed it over the years as an adult, but for now, I just sat there staring at him.

"You're family," he said. "I made extra just for you. Come, pull up a chair!"

Cautiously, I went over to the table. Michael shot me a confused look. His head was stooped toward his plate as he held his fork inches away from its target, gravy dripping from the side of his mouth. "Dude, what's wrong with you? Free food! Eat!"

I sat down and ate my meal with my best manners, even though it was undoubtedly the best biscuits and gravy I'd ever had. Bob cooked chunks of sausage in the gravy and the biscuits were fresh and flaky! After I finished, I thanked him and gathered my things to head back home.

"My pleasure, Christopher," he smiled, cleaning the stove, "stay as long as you want."

The Hyde house was slowly becoming my new refuge, a place to escape life at home. It gave me a familiar feeling that made me warm up to Coldwater. Maybe it wouldn't be so bad, at least until I could return to Danielle.

The Hydes treated me with respect. Bob asked my opinion on things and never put me down. But what truly struck me about him was that he seemed the true antithesis to my father. He rarely yelled, only raising his voice sternly on occasion. He and Aunt Bonnie never argued, at least not in front of the kids.

The biggest difference between Bob and my father was how he treated his wife. He was completely in love with Aunt Bonnie, and he wasn't afraid to say it. She was his world. He wasn't too proud to be romantic, telling us that real men have the courage to fall in love.

"I love my wife. If anyone doesn't like it, they can kiss my ass."

Part of me wanted to tell them about Danielle because it was hard keeping it to myself. But I restrained myself. Not yet. It was too personal. The last thing I needed was to hear the "there's no way she still loves you" argument. I couldn't risk it.

I'd developed the habit of calling Danielle almost every other day. Just like we talked back in Florida, we shared with each other all our thoughts, feelings, and the details of our lives. These phone calls were the best part of my life.

And then they stopped.

I kept her phone number on a blue piece of paper, clipped to the inside of the address book on the living room table. I always put it in the same place for fear of losing her information. I'll never know why I didn't just commit it to memory.

The day came when I went to call her, and the paper wasn't there. Frantically, I searched through every page of the book twice. I picked it up by the spine and shook it. I looked through the table drawer, the entire floor, as well under the furniture.

For over two hours, I searched in panic. I was now very late for my phone call with her. I had no way of telling her I hadn't forgotten about her. All the while, Dick sat in his armchair nearby, ignoring me while watching his westerns on TV.

Finally, Mom walked in, home from work. "What's wrong?" she asked when she saw me losing my mind.

"I can't find Danielle's number! I was supposed to call her hours ago!"

"Calm down," she said, going over to the same drawer I'd already destroyed. "I'm sure it's somewhere around here." She helped me for a few minutes, but eventually gave up and left. By then, I was a complete wreck. My temper was flaring when Dick finally spoke up, thrusting a finger in my direction.

"You better calm down right now," he demanded.

"I can't!" I snapped back, "I need to find her number!"

"You're not going to because I threw it away."

"You what?"

"I threw it away. You ran up our phone bill last month. I told you not to do that shit!"

My blood pressure skyrocketed. In my mind, I saw myself taking the pen next to his chair and stabbing him in the throat with it over and over.

"You better calm your scrawny ass down before I beat you." He leaned forward in his chair and grimaced at me, daring me to do something. "You wanna go? Mommy isn't here to protect you. That girl was over you before we even left. She's probably had four different boyfriends by now. You two are done!"

I found myself in familiar territory. I wanted to hit him as hard as I could. I wanted to put my fist through his face! But I reminded myself that Danielle's man wouldn't hit him. Danielle would never tolerate someone who starts violence.

I needed to get out of there. It was vital that I go somewhere as far away from him as possible before I lost control. I was on the brink of doing something stupid.

Michael welcomed me as I stormed into the Hyde house, slamming the door behind me. I dragged him downstairs and unloaded.

My fury echoed throughout their house. I was about to explode in equal parts anger and tears. I imagined Danielle sitting by the phone, pissed at me for not calling when I said I would. I imagined her feeling worse and worse as more days passed with no word from me. She probably thought I forgot about her. I imagined everything Dick said coming true. He had taken her phone number away from me, and, by extension, her.

"Dang, dude. Do you wanna go for a bike ride?" Michael clearly wasn't used to this kind of emotion. "Maybe it'll help you calm down."

Begrudgingly, I agreed, and we rode across town to a small video game store called Gamers Heaven. The distraction did me good, but an hour later, arriving back at his house, I saw Dick's car in the driveway.

Great.

Of course, Bob's friendliness with our family extended to Dick, and as two adult men they naturally grew closer. Just another reason for me to distrust the guy. The two of them were sitting on the side porch. I matched Dick's stare as Michael and I dropped our bikes at the end of the driveway. We walked up to the front without saying a word.

But no sooner than we entered the house, we heard yelling coming from outside. We stopped in our tracks to see what was going on, but could only see shadows moving beyond the kitchen curtains. Just as soon as it started, it stopped. We waited, frozen, expecting the door to fling open in a fury, but nothing happened. Then I recognized Dick's cursing. A car door slammed, and tires peeled away.

Michael looked at me, shrugged, and went downstairs. But I opened the back door to see what had happened.

Bob was there alone, sitting in a porch chair and watching the squirrels running around the yard. His leg was bouncing up and down restlessly. I walked out and quietly leaned against the rail.

"I'm sorry, Christopher." Bob said suddenly.

I turned to look at him. "For what?"

He took a deep breath.

"Well, I just cussed out your stepdad, son. He came over screaming and yelling about some phone bill. I mean, I don't care about it, honestly. I figured he was just blowing off steam. But he started calling you names when you guys come home."

"What did he say?"

Bob was hesitant to answer. After a moment, he cleared his throat. "He called you a 'fucking little cocksucker,'" he said without looking at me. "I'm sorry," he blurted out after a pause, "I shouldn't have told you that. But I heard about how bad your dad was, and then hearing that…" He looked at me again. "I just want you to know that you don't deserve to be spoken about like that, ever."

It shocked me to see how upset he was.

"Look," he began, "I see how you're still not comfortable with me and I get it. I mean, I think I know why." I stayed quiet, curious about what he would say next.

"I go telling you, 'Hey, I'm your dad's best friend,' and you think that means I'm just like him, or that maybe I caused him to turn out the way he did, am I right? Well, I want you to know that I am nothing like what you think about me. After we left Korea, and that was 1953, we went our separate ways. He wasn't like that when I saw him last. That was not the man I knew. I mean, his dad, your granddad, he was rough. I could see how your grandfather could've really screwed him up. Back then, he was determined not to be like his dad, and last I knew him, he wasn't. Then you guys came along."

His hand gripped the armrest of his chair. I could see his knuckles going pale.

Then, lowering his tone solemnly, he added, "I am sorry for all of it. You deserve better, kid. What he did to you guys was unforgivable. Dick seems like he's maybe only a little better. In your life, you have had enough shit to deal with. You're still just a boy! You need a man you can look up to. You need—" His restrained emotion was causing him to tremble. "You *don't* deserve to be treated like that."

He leaned in toward me, making this intense moment even more so. "I know we've only known each other for a few months now, but just know that I will not stand for it. Someone must stick up for you, and I'm happy to do it."

I looked away. No man had ever talked to me like this before. I didn't know how to receive it. Then I asked, "So what did you say to him?"

Bob chuckled, "I told Dick that if I ever heard him talk to or about my nephew like that ever again, I'd kick his ass. He stormed off after that. Something tells me I shouldn't expect any more invitations to your house for a while."

I could only stare ahead, incredulous, as his words sunk in. This man, this stranger, stood up for me? To Dick? I did not know what to say. I was speechless.

"Thanks," was all I could muster.

"Whatever you need, I'm here for you. I want to help you every way I can. We're your family, do you understand? You will always have a place with us. And I will always have your back, no matter what."

I nodded and smiled, holding back tears. I started believing him. He wasn't like my father at all. He might've even been the exact opposite of my father: a good man.

"But I gotta know something," he continued in a more casual tone, bringing relief to the moment, "who were you calling to run up the phone bill like that?"

Only one second had passed since I trusted this man, and the first thing he did was test that trust. I answered cautiously, "A girl I know back home."

Bob's face twisted into a huge grin. "She cute?"

"She's the most beautiful girl ever."

He pointed at the pendant hanging over my t-shirt. "I take it that's her?"

I nodded. He reached over and playfully smacked me on the knee. "She must be one hell of a girl."

I tried to hide my smile but couldn't. It was nice being able to talk about my feelings with an adult who didn't immediately tell me they were wrong. My gut was telling me I was safe with Bob. I could trust him. He was good.

"So, Michael tells me you want to learn Karate," he said, changing the subject.

"Yeah. But Mom says no. She's afraid if I learn to fight, I'm going to turn out like my dad. But she tells me all the time I'm going to turn out like him anyway, so I don't see what difference it makes."

Bob let out a vast sigh. "Martial arts did not make your father what he is. Your granddad did some unspeakable shit to him. Martial arts can help you conquer your demons, to take control of them, make them better, not worse."

"I need to protect myself," I blurted out in frustration. "I've been beaten up my entire life. I don't want to hurt anyone; I just want to stop people from hurting me. I need to protect those I love."

"You mean your girl?" He grinned.

I looked him square in the eyes and nodded. "Danielle."

"Confidence building, hmm? Sounds like you're a great candidate for Michael's class. They meet on Tuesdays and Thursdays."

He made it sound so easy. Just walk in and sign up. "It doesn't matter," I said. "Mom won't let me. I've already tried."

Bob reached over and put his hand on my shoulder. "You need to learn how to protect yourself. Leave your mother to me. I promise she'll see things our way."

Our way? I'm really liking this guy.

"What happens if she still says no?"

He flashed me a devilish smile. "Then I'll teach you myself!"

I laughed and relaxed comfortably onto the porch rail, the two of us side by side, watching the squirrels dart around the lawn. He squeezed my shoulder, and for the first time I didn't flinch when another man touched me.

• •

True to form, Bob showed up at our front door the next day around noon. Dick stayed in the living room. I ran upstairs to let him work his charm on my mother. The last thing I wanted to do was interfere at all and risk ruining his work. *I guess I do trust him*; I realized.

While I wasn't privy to the exact conversation, I could make out muffled sounds coming from where they were. At some point, it sounded like Mom raised her voice, but he seemed to keep his cool because his volume never shifted.

Ten minutes rolled by. Then twenty. It became harder to hear them since Dick turned up the television in the living room. I was getting anxious. Was Bob successful? I knew in my heart that if he couldn't convince her, I'd be in trouble for his even trying.

I headed downstairs. Not knowing how things went was driving me crazy. I entered the dining room to see the two of them sitting at the dinner table. Mom was the first to notice me, and I froze in my tracks.

"Sit down," she said. I lowered myself onto the chair opposite her. Her jaw tensed as she strummed her fingers on the table.

"I'm going to step outside for a few minutes while you two talk," Bob said, patting me on the shoulder as he left.

We just sat there, the silence becoming painful. Slowly, my mother shifted her gaze up to me, her nostrils flaring.

"Your uncle and I have just had an interesting talk," she began. I stayed absolutely silent, my eyes wide with unease.

"Apparently, he knows about our conversations about you wanting to take karate. He knows, in very specific detail, how I feel about it."

Her face was turning red. I knew my mother better than anyone. She wanted to explode, but was holding back. I didn't know how much longer she would be able to.

"Let me be clear. I don't appreciate our affairs being advertised outside of this house. I have my reasons for not wanting you to get into that kind of thing, and I don't appreciate having third parties stick their noses into our business. And I told your uncle as much."

My restraint waned. "Your reasons! You won't let me because you're afraid I'll end up like my father. I won't!"

She held her hand up to stop me.

"I have seen how you've changed since we left Florida. You are angry about leaving Danielle. I know why you wear that necklace. I'm telling you right now, if you are doing all of this, learning karate, wearing jewelry for her in some hope that she will take you back someday, you are *wasting* the best years of your life for someone who probably won't even remember you. You're getting older and you need to make some serious choices. All it takes is one poor decision to ruin your life."

I clenched my jaw as hard as I could, suspiciously hopeful.

"But your uncle apparently agrees with you, about you not being like your dad," she said, shifting gears. "he told me he would take full responsibility if you hurt anyone. I want to believe both of you. I do, Chris. But I still have my reservations. I'm a mother, you know. I worry."

She took a deep breath. "I know you don't believe it, but I do have some idea of how unfair this has all been for you. Your father, the hearing, moving to Michigan, what happened to Ryan." She listed the tragedies of my life like they were pantry items on a grocery list.

My hands were tightening into fists inside the pockets of my jeans. *Here it comes. She's not going to let me.*

"Despite my feelings, I don't want to add another thing to the list of reasons you're angry. So, I'm going to let you take classes with Michael—as a trial."

At that moment, the room lit up around me like a Christmas spectacular. *Is this real?*

"But make no mistake," she continued rigidly, "the first time I hear you hurt someone outside of class, you are done. Done! Are we clear?"

I lunged forward and hugged her face. "Thank you!" I squealed. "Thank you, Mom!" She smiled and patted my arm. "And, Mom, I will not hurt anyone outside of class. I'm not my father."

I ran outside where Uncle Bob was standing and clutched him in a massive hug. He chuckled and accepted me full force.

"I guess the conversation went well?"

"Yes!" I shouted. I hadn't felt that happy since Florida.

"Looks like you're all set, then."

"I can't believe you did this for me!" I said, almost crying.

"A man keeps his word, Chris. See you on Tuesday."

2,225 days remaining...

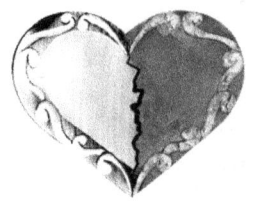

18

"You're the Best Around"
(by Joe Esposito)

The next day, Uncle Bob and Michael picked me up for my first karate class. I was nervous he might not show up, but the Chevy pulled into our driveway right on time. "A man always keeps his word," he said with a wink, sensing my distress as I ran out of the house.

Still, I couldn't shake my foul mood as we left the house. I'd been feeling worse and worse about not being able to talk to Danielle. In our last conversation, she'd told me that her family had also moved away from Fairhaven Street to the other side of town. Her dad told her to get off the phone before she could give me the new address, so I couldn't even write her a letter. The reality of our severed connection became heavier with every hour. As I waited by the door, waiting for Uncle Bob, Dick taunted me from his armchair. "This won't last long," he chuckled to himself. "As soon as it gets hard, you'll quit like you quit everything you've ever started."

When we arrived at class, I realized I was the only one in a group of five who was dressed in street clothes. As the other students followed the rituals of lining up and bowing, I faltered behind awkwardly. I had never been involved with any kind of physical activity, sport or otherwise, and it was brutally obvious here at the Sanchin-Ryu Karate program. I felt terrible, and everyone could see it.

Gary, my new sensei, tried to put me at ease with a compassionate smile as I explained why I was not dressed appropriately. He was a stocky gentleman with blue eyes and a blond mullet. "Don't worry, I'm sure you'll get your *Gi* soon enough."

His friendliness and patience with me continued as he taught me a basic punch. His arm whipped out so quickly it was a blur. I stood in front of him in disbelief that a human being could move that fast.

"Now you try," he said. I just stood there in my blue jeans and t-shirt, clutching one arm with the other. "Go on, Chris," he encouraged. "Try it." I jutted out my arm quickly into the air in front of me. No power at all.

"Try again," he said. "You'll get it. Just relax your fist as you extend your arm out until just before you hit your target."

He corrected my form as he spoke. "Imagine going through the target a full inch."

The other students, Janice, Pam, and Michael did their best to encourage me as well, but I had a bad habit of beating myself up for not getting it right away. Many times throughout that class, I wanted to quit. I could hear my father's voice screaming in my head.

"You're pathetic. You can't even throw a punch right! Just give up, C.J. Quit! That's what you're going to end up doing, anyway. Why delay the inevitable?"

Yet, despite my flailing arms and self-destructive mindset, in those moments I learned the enormous power that came with a will fueled by rage. Instead of following the words of both my father and Dick and giving in, I pushed forward. When Gary told me to practice ten punches, I did twenty. Gary gave me a nod of praise as the class continued.

The flip side to using anger as a motivator bit me in the ass soon enough. I squared up with someone to spar and, in my mind, where they stood also stood every single person who decided it was their right to pick on me. I saw the contempt for me on their faces and heard nasty words dripping from their tongues. This was my chance to begin the journey to become the man who she would want to be with. I needed to keep moving forward.

I lunged forward with all my might, charging like a furious bull, throwing each strike as if it were my last. I went in raging and ended up doubled over and gasping for air as a foot entered my gut.

"Take your time," Gary said, helping me over to a chair. "Don't go in so hot. Remember, we're not trying to hurt anyone. Karate is for self-defense only!"

"I'm sorry," I said, catching my breath.

He sat down next to me. "You don't need to apologize. It's okay to make mistakes. Mistakes are how we get better. But you seem angry, Chris."

"Yes sir," I confirmed, but offered nothing more.

"Look. Just focus on breathing and visualize what you're trying to do in your mind. Always do that before acting. And relax! Nobody here expects you to be perfect. You just started!"

I nodded.

"Let's try again. Go against me this time. Also, you'll need to take off that necklace during class."

"I can't do that, sir."

He stopped and looked at me.

"It's probably going to get torn off by accident. You wear that all the time?"

I nodded.

"Okay, well, tuck it under your shirt, then."

I did as I was told and followed him onto the mat to spar. I relaxed more and visualized my movements in my mind beforehand. Even though he kept knocking me down on my ass, I found it strangely calming.

I wasn't sure if Gary was taking it easy on me or something clicked, but after a while, I could avoid getting hit. We went back and forth, exchanging, blocking, and moving. He smiled after we finished.

"See what happens when you relax more? Great job!"

He was right. Forcing myself to relax allowed me to think quickly and adapt. We squared off again, and he came in swinging. While I eventually got "hit"—he threw a strike that stopped just shy of contact—I could avoid other strikes. The only strike that got me was an improvisation he did that I had no counter for—yet.

The hour flew by, and my first class was done. Gary and Michael sat down with me as they got their shoes on.

"Great job, man!" Michael said, patting me on the back. I flinched a little as he did it, which Gary noticed. Michael cleared his throat and excused himself as he ran over to Janice and Pam.

Gary smiled as he grabbed his bags.

"He's right, you know. You did a great job today."

"Thank you."

"But listen," he went on as we all filed out, "don't be so hard on yourself. Just keep trying. You'll get it. Life is about little victories. Keep your focus on the little things and your ability will improve. And about that anger of yours. Anger can be a powerful tool, but you need to learn to control it before it can be useful."

I looked at him as he threw his bag over his shoulder and headed to his truck. "Don't give up. I promise, this will be good for you if you stick with it."

He waved goodbye as everyone else came over and congratulated me. Michael nudged me as we began our trip home.

"Not bad for your first day!"

• •

My first few weeks of karate lessons, I focused entirely on the punch. This single movement changed my entire way of thinking. One skilled punch became, for me, a symbol of power. I felt that if I could learn to punch properly and powerfully, I could do anything. I would prove to myself that anything can be overcome with persistence.

I'd throw punch after punch against a pillow I duct-taped to the wall. (Dick refused to buy a punching bag, referring to karate as "kung fooey bullshit.") I felt no power when I hit it. I hit that pillow repeatedly.

Gary did his best to correct my form, but he could see how easily frustrated I got. Uncle Bob offered advice as well. On the days he came to class to watch us, I tried even harder to do my best. I wanted to impress him, especially since he was the one who bought me my *gi* after my parents refused.

"Put your hip into it, Christopher!" Uncle Bob would yell. "Drive it forward with the hip, not just the shoulder."

"Keep trying," Gary would add. "I know it doesn't seem like it now, but one day it will all click. Everything will fall into place, and it will become second nature."

Back at home, I kept punching that pillow. Day and night. I was waiting for this training to beat back the voice of my father, but to my surprise, it only grew louder.

"Can't even punch right... pathetic little weakling."

The more I heard it, the more determined I became. Each time I started on another round of strikes, I touched Danielle's pendant, not for luck, but to remind me of my purpose. I felt like I was failing her. I punched and punched, trying to use the anger to create the power I wanted.

In my mind I saw the fear on Danielle's face that day those four boys jumped us, which now felt like a lifetime ago. I remembered the sense of urgency to do whatever it took to protect her. I remembered how powerless I felt on my bike, heading home.

Then that same voice from Ryan's funeral came thundering back. *Fuck that shit! Quit feeling sorry for yourself and take control! One day, you are going to have to protect her again, and this time, you'll be ready. That pillow is stopping you from getting the life you want! DESTROY IT!*

But my punches failed to break past the soft inside of the pillow. They barely made a sound. My knuckles could make just enough contact with the wall to make them red and swollen, but not enough for success.

Ten times, twenty times, forty times, I kept hitting. All the searing anger I felt toward my parents, the desire I felt to become what I knew I could become, the emptiness that came with almost three years of being alone. I focused everything on that simple movement.

Until one day, it happened.

WHACK!

The wall shook as my punch went through the pillow and hit the stud behind it. I looked at my hand in disbelief.

Holy shit! Did I just do that?

Then I heard footsteps coming up the stairs.

"What the hell are you doing up there?" Dick yelled.

I laughed in disbelief. For the first time in my life, I felt powerful. I now could cause serious damage.

I had to do it again to be sure I hadn't dreamed it. I hauled off and put my body into it as one unit.

WHACK!

This one shook part of the house.

"Knock it off or I'll come up there and kick your ass!"

Now I was laughing for an entirely different reason. No way would Dick stand a chance of getting hit with that kind of power. He'd be destroyed, and by a scrawny kid too.

I radiated with an incredible sense of pride. My entire world changed with that one little victory. I broke through all my self-doubt and had the sudden realization that the same approach could work in other arenas in my life as well. For the first time, I could see myself becoming that man who would return to Florida and take back my destiny.

What started as one little victory led to another, which boosted my confidence just a little more. Over time, it continued to another, and another, and another. The more I accomplished, the more my confidence grew.

It bled into every part of my life. After a while, my exploits became more and more difficult. I was drifting further and further away from C.J., the boy who was barely tolerated, who quit everything he started.

After a time, it was as if that boy was just a dot on the horizon. Achievement became like a drug, and I couldn't get enough of the high that came with it.

I was unstoppable.

Back at Sanchin-Ryu, Gary kept working with me to change my view of my anger. For so long my mother focused only on eliminating it, fearfully. Gary explained that the only way to harness the power inside of anger was to embrace it, to accept it as a part of me. With his guidance, I learned to take control of it to use it as fuel throughout my life. It was anger that pushed me forward when I wanted to quit, to do what needed to be done when everyone else was complaining. It was better to use it for something useful than for something destructive.

That punch led me to learn other techniques, and along with them, the martial arts philosophy. Over five years, I moved up in rank: white belt, green, orange, purple, and finally three levels of brown. Eventually, Michael and Janice received their black belts, leaving me as the last one without it.

It thrilled Uncle Bob, watching me move up. He saw how I stood up taller than before, how I looked him in the eye more and more. I overheard him bragging about how I would soon join "the club," a.k.a. the Black Belt Club, just like he and my father had so long ago. He boasted about me to others like I was his own son.

When Dick would occasionally refuse to pay for my classes, Uncle Bob and Gary paid for me under the table, or so I found out from Pam some years later. I approached Uncle Bob and asked him if it was true. He simply nodded.

"You're worth the money."

Uncle Bob did more than support me in karate. He taught me how to talk to women, how to walk confidently, or as he would put it, "move like you've got a purpose." I learned the art of charming a woman.

He continued to show me that a man can be completely in love with his wife and still be badass.

If I'm even a quarter of the man he is when I grow up, it will be a monumental accomplishment.

Gary, Pam, Michael, Janice, and Uncle Bob would become a second family—my Sanchin family. They would be there throughout all the difficulties in my journey back to Florida.

I was lucky to have my Sanchin family because I was about to enter one of the most challenging parts of life: high school. I needed all the help I could get.

2,224 days remaining...

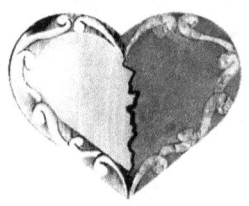

19

"Fight Song"
(by Sister Sin)

Coldwater High School, home of the Fighting Cardinals. For many teenagers in such a small town, school was the epicenter of their lives. For me, it was just a pit stop, a prelude to finally going home.

I quickly learned that while high school differs from middle school, in some respects, it's the same. I entered with the intent of yet another fresh start. I was going to be more outgoing and more sociable.

But some things never change.

On the first day, I was reminded that I did not have the personality to overcome being unfortunate looking. As soon as we assembled in the gym for freshman orientation, the cliques formed. My efforts to be friendly were met with varying degrees of awkwardness or rudeness until I was left standing alone again.

So, I did what I did best. I retreated into myself and became my own island. I ate lunch by myself. Blending into the background of everyday life became a regular occurrence.

Six months passed and still no one knew my name. Occasionally, someone would ask me about the pendant, only to go about their business after I declined to answer. I was just the weird guy with the necklace.

My participation in school life consisted mostly of inadvertent eavesdropping. Sitting in a large classroom with a group of people all day made one privy to scuttlebutt. The conversations I found most interesting were the girls complaining about the boys.

"Why are guys such jerks?"

"Why can't I get a good-looking guy to go out with me?"

"Why can't high school boys commit to a relationship? They all just want to get laid, and that's it."

They didn't even notice me as I listened nearby, keeping my comments to myself. All I could do was roll my eyes. They did not know about my history until the beginning of the holiday season.

Mr. Bailey had given us an assignment to write a short poem about someone we cared about. Picking my muse was easy, and I didn't have any trouble with the writing, either. But at the end of the week, we had to endure the dreadful task of reading our poems in front of the entire class.

I considered writing a decoy poem, debating whether to expose my heart to yet another new group of kids who would no doubt reject me. But part of me wanted these girls to hear it. I wanted them to see that they might find someone great if they could get past superficial things like appearances.

The day came, and one by one, each student read their poem. Some spoke about their parents, many about friends, boyfriends, some even wrote about their siblings. One kid even wrote about her cat, which got a good chuckle from the audience.

True to form, I was the next-to-last to be called up. My feet felt heavy as I rose from the back of the class, and my heart pounded as I slowly made my way to the front of the room. I clutched the paper in front of me as I squared myself to my executioners. Every single eye in that room burned through me as I cleared my throat and read.

I wish I had a copy of that poem saved to share here with you, boys, but all that remains is the memory of it. All I can recall now is the last line of it, as it was the clincher. "I worry about where I'll go when I die.

To me, heaven is a life spent with you, so where does that leave me when I go?"

The guys yawned and rolled their eyes, but the girls looked amazed, almost dumbfounded. They gazed upon me as if they had seen a ghost: the ghost of men-they-didn't-realize-existed. I could hear the faint whispers of the complainers from before, the same lamenters wanting romance in their simple lives. No doubt they were now wondering, "Who is this guy? Who is this mystery girl?"

The half-ass applause that followed the other presentations was absent when mine concluded. As Uncle Bob would say, "It was so quiet you could hear a church mouse piss on a cotton ball." All twenty-odd students, including Mr. Bailey, just stared at me. The only sound came from a car pulling out of the parking lot right outside the window.

"Pussy!" one of the popular guys coughed from the back of the room. The other guys roared with laughter, but the girls yelled and glared at them, telling them to shut up. My face went a shade redder, my poem hanging at my side.

Mr. Bailey seemed either deep in thought or deeply concerned. He sat in his chair nearby, his arms crossed. He seemed at a loss for words, which was rare. "Wow," he finally said. "That was... interesting, Chris."

I quietly made my way back to my desk, every female eye following me.

The girl sitting in front of me turned around to look at me when I got to my seat. "That's why you're wearing that pendant, isn't it?" she said excitedly. "For *her*."

I gave a small smile. Some girls looked around at each other. One guy pretended to throw up.

After class, four of the girls approached me to ask more questions about Danielle.

"What's her favorite flower?" asked a tall brunette.

"Gerbera Daisies."

"Figures," she returned. "My boyfriend can't even remember my last name, let alone my favorite flower."

"What's her birthday?" asked a shorter redhead.

"June thirtieth."

They all gushed again.

"Are you going to go after her?"

"After we graduate, I'm going to go back for her."

Then the redhead came up close to me and took my glasses off. The gaggle of girls closed in around me.

"Oh my God," she said, "you should totally get contacts. I bet she'd love it!" The others all agreed. "Your eyes are gorgeous. What are they, green?"

I took a step backward and bumped into a locker. "Yeah. They're hazel. They change with my mood. The green in them only shows when I'm happy."

"So, your eyes must have always been green when you were around her."

I stopped and considered what she had just said.

"I don't think she even realized they were hazel."

The redhead carefully put my glasses back on my face and flashed an approving smile.

The sound of the school bell suddenly echoed down the hall. They all waved goodbye and dispersed to their next class. I stood in place, still trying to convince myself that everything in the last twenty minutes had happened. That was the most female attention I'd ever received.

And I really liked it.

The guys in my class were a different story. The poem only made them like me even less. Before, I was the weird, quiet kid. Now I was the weird kid who had made them look bad in front of the girls.

At first, the consequence was just taunting from afar. A derogatory name yelled in my direction from down the hall. I always assumed the taunting I got would be minimal since I was a six-foot-tall freshman. But over time, the taunts became more direct.

There was one thin, blond guy named Eric, a sophomore, who took it upon himself to bully me. He and his group of four friends had quickly built a reputation for picking on the younger students. It wasn't unusual to see him shove someone into a locker or yank someone else into the boys' bathroom. Until that point, they had not bothered me.

Then one day, as we all bustled through the hall between classes, a bony elbow jabbed me, knocking me against the lockers and causing my books to crash to the floor. I let it roll off my back as best I could. After all, we ignore bullies, and they will go away, right?

Wrong again, Mom.

Once I started ignoring him, he doubled his efforts. At lunch, he would fling food at me. After school, he'd shoot spitballs at me. And then one day, when our teacher stepped out of class, Eric seized his opportunity to take things to the next level.

"Look at that freak over there, sitting by himself. Hey freak, how's your make-believe girlfriend in Florida?"

I ignored him, but the mention of Danielle sparked my temper. At this point, I'd been at Sanchin Ryu for a few months and was trying to keep my nose clean. If I got into a fight, I knew my parents wouldn't let me go back.

"Come on, pussy. You take karate now, right? You think you're some kind of badass? Try that shit with me and I'll fucking wipe the floor with your ugly ass."

My tolerance was wearing thin. I had already punched through the pillow by this point, so I was becoming less tolerant of crap. I turned and shot him a nasty look.

"You wanna go? Make a move, bitch!"

I returned my attention to the television playing in the classroom's front. He started flinging rubber bands at me. One hit me in the back of the head. He and his buddies erupted in stupid laughter.

Still, I kept my cool.

"Are you writing another letter to your fake girlfriend?"

Getting hotter.

"You know what? I think she is real. I think she's totally real. A real whore cunt!"

I shot up to my feet, my desk careening forward and smashing into the teacher's area. The entire class fell completely silent as they stared.

I couldn't defend her when I was younger, but I was damn sure going to do it now. It didn't matter if she'd never hear the words he said. It was a matter of honor. I remembered what Gary said as I stared at him. *Defense only.*

He snorted with laughter as I came up to him.

"Ooh boy! I found his weakness, guys! He can't accept the fact that his girlfriend is a big slut."

But his tough-guy attitude faded away as I spoke. "Get your ass up right now."

His face shifted to concern, though he tried desperately to play it off. "Watch out, guys! Freshman here is gonna karate chop my ass!" He threw some chops in the air and wrongly attempted to yell *kiai*.

"I said get your little weasel ass up."

I felt like I was outside of my body, watching everything go down. My mind went completely red. I didn't know this person who looked like me. Eric finally eased off his bully charade.

"Why should I?" he scoffed.

"Hit me. I'll give you the first shot."

"W... what? Get out of here, freak."

"You said you'd wipe the floor with my ass. Do it. Take the first shot."

"You take the first shot, freak!"

"But then you'll be knocked out. I want you to swing at me."

"Why?"

"Because what I'm about to do to you needs to be in self-defense."

Time stood still. Now Eric was silent. He looked at his friends, who looked just as clueless as he was. Slowly, they came to and egged him on.

"Come on, Eric! Do it! Kick his ass! He doesn't know shit."

"Yeah, Eric!"

He looked at me sideways.

"N... no," he responded. "You're not worth it."

"Come on, Eric," I said, remaining calm and towering over him. "You heard your friends. I don't know shit. Step up."

He nervously shifted in his seat.

"No!" he shouted. "Not here. Outside, after school. Meet me between the football field and the gym today at three. I'll beat your ass then."

I smiled as he relaxed. He'd saved his reputation for the time being.

"See you then," I said and moved my desk back to its place.

• •

The bell rang at 2:55. Five minutes later, I was at the agreed-upon spot. A thin blanket of snow had coated the ground, covering the markings on the field next to me.

Part of me knew this was ridiculous. This wasn't self-defense, no matter how I tried to twist it. There was no way Gary would condone this. But I'd had enough of Eric's behavior. I was sick of bullies, sick of getting picked on. Ignoring them never worked. Some people can't be reasoned with. The only way to stop them is to physically engage with them. Violence is their only dialect.

I understood the adamant adherence to the self-defense-only philosophy, but I watched other kids get tormented day in and day out with no one helping them, I wondered, *What's the point of having a skill if you don't use it to help others?*

I soaked the inner linings of my winter gloves in sweat. My mind was in a tug-of-war between *This is not right* and *This has to be done*. For all I knew, this could turn into a five-on-one fight. For all I knew, they could be carrying weapons.

A few minutes later, Eric showed up with his group. He seemed even more nervous than before, despite his crew smacking him on the back for encouragement. My internal tug of war was finished.

This must be done.

I watched as he tried to psych himself up. I had the rest of my life to avoid fighting, but not this day. Not this fight. We were past the point of no return.

"Okay. Let's go!" he yelled, trying to get himself excited. He shifted his weight back and forth, glaring at me like a boxer trying to convince himself he wasn't risking brain damage.

I only smiled at him and brought my right foot back slightly to open my stance, a typical karate move before launching an attack. My arms were down by my side, but I was ready. I knew that bringing my arms up in a fighting position could be construed as a threat, and I didn't want him to back down. This was happening, whether or not he wanted it to.

"Hit me," I said.

He remained hesitant. My patience was now razor thin. The longer we took, the more likely an adult was going to see us and stop it.

"I said hit me! Quit being a bitch!"

"Ooh," his buddies said collectively.

Eric's face was now twitching.

"Come on," I kept going. "You talk nonstop about how you could kick my ass. Now's your chance to prove it. Or are you just full of shit?"

His face turned red. His jaw clenched. He advanced.

Adrenaline coursed through my body. I was scared, but focused. I figured he would be a headhunter, someone whose sole focus on a fight was to constantly aim for the head. The untrained usually are.

Hold it steady. DON'T KILL HIM!

I was right. He came in with a wide-arching right hook.

Thirty seconds later, the fight was over. It was sloppy. It was ugly. Real-life fights never look as good as they do in training.

I let him land his first punch, and I've got to admit he got a second one in, too. But I stayed calm and focused as I finally got my answer to the question of how much damage a punch that could shake a wall could do to a live person.

His legs gave out, causing him to sink down to the ground as soon as I contacted his temple. One hit was all it took. I remember hearing a sickening *smack* as I hit him clean. Luckily, he didn't hit his head on the pavement as he went down.

With surprising strength, I picked up his limp body and locked him in a rear naked choke. He grabbed my arm, trying to pull it off, snorting; the steam from his breath rose in front of my face and mixed with mine as it floated to the sky.

His friends screamed for him to stomp my feet. I coiled my right arm around his neck, but I wasn't applying any pressure. I just wanted to scare him. I wanted to scare all of them so that no one would ever mess with me again.

Sure enough, he struggled and tried stomping at my feet.

"Eric," I said disapprovingly, "if you do that again, I'm going to choke you for real. Tap out."

He relaxed, but still refused to tap. I thought he was just holding out before complying. I was wrong. Suddenly, he slammed his heel down onto my right foot. It hurt, but not enough for me to relinquish the hold.

I dropped my weight onto my back, taking him with me. As soon as we hit the ground, my arm closed around his neck, cutting off his air supply. His arms waved frantically, trying to hit me in the face, but to no avail. Within a few seconds, his arms dropped lifelessly to his sides, and I released the hold. I was in control, and I wasn't about to kill anyone. That was the last thing I wanted to do.

Pushing him off of me, I got to my feet and faced his crew, panting. The adrenaline was still coursing through my veins. I was ready to take on anyone else who dared try me. I was a new person now, a person who would not take shit from anyone anymore, ever.

They looked at each other nervously.

"He... he deserved it!" one yelled emphatically.

"Yeah! That was fucked up what he said to you, Chris!"

"I always believed you about her!"

I looked over as Eric began coming to. I knelt down next to him and spoke calmly as he rolled to his side.

"Never insult Danielle again."

He nodded as he rubbed his head.

I turned and walked inside to grab my things. My soul lit up with pride. I wasn't proud of myself for beating him up, only that I had finally stood up for myself.

Eric would be okay. I would be okay as well. No one was going to jail. I remember walking home that day feeling the best I had in a long time. Inevitably, word would get around, and that would be enough to secure my new reputation. I was glad there were no other witnesses.

After that day, I was never bullied at school ever again.

Home was still a different subject, for now.

2,210 days remaining...

20

"In This Life"
(by Chantal Kreviazuk)

The van's dashboard read seventy-two degrees, but my hands were sweating so badly I could hardly control the steering wheel. I had whittled two thousand miles down to the last two. My breath left my body as I entered her driveway.

I parked and just sat there, trying to muster the courage to get out. The vehicle shook gently as it idled. I was shaking as well, trying to cool down in the blasting air conditioning. The Florida sun beat down on me through the glass as my mind raced.

This needs to be perfect. I need to be perfect. I only get one shot.

After a few minutes, I paused and turned off the engine. I closed my eyes, counted to three, and forced the door open to the world. My feet landed heavily on the driveway, interrupting the song of a nearby scrub jay. I worried he was calling out a warning that I'd arrived, and I tried in vain to quiet him.

I caught my reflection in the side mirror. Here I was, the man I'd always wanted to be. I gelled my hair into a stylish mess. I wore contacts instead of glasses. My jaw had developed a strong geometry, chiseled almost, something that actually looked pretty good. It was like looking at myself for the first time.

Am I good-looking? I wondered in amazement. *I'm good-looking! I'm good-looking!*

Smiling, I reached through the van's open window and pulled out an enormous bouquet of multi-colored Gerber daisies. Then I began the trek up the waterlogged driveway, edged with red rose bushes, as the scrub jay continued its warning.

Standing in front of a large oak door with a brass handle—it was then that I felt it. It was something I hadn't felt in years.

Butterflies.

They smashed against the insides of my stomach, trying desperately to break free. I felt nauseous. There was only one person who'd ever made me feel this way. Only one person existed who would compel me to drive two thousand miles with little sleep.

All I had to do was reach out and press the doorbell and my life would change forever. All those years practicing what I was going to say when the time came and I saw her again had led to this very moment. Suddenly, I felt like a coward again.

My feet were frozen to the step, my arm refusing to raise my hand to touch the bell. Why did I hesitate to take the last step of my thousand-year journey?

Screw it, I thought. *I deserve to be happy. I've been through hell. The life on the other side of this door is mine.*

DING DONG!

The breath left my body as I heard the lock turning. The door swung open to reveal my future.

"Oh my God... Chris? Is it really you?"

I was beyond speechless. She was no longer the most beautiful girl I'd ever seen. Standing before me was the most beautiful woman in the world. Her hair was just below her shoulders, darker than I remembered, but still shining in the light as it had done before, resting in a perfect frame around her face.

Her cheekbones had grown more pronounced. Her button nose grew in proportion with her face, just as cute as always. And her eyes still sparkled that mesmerizing bright emerald, now staring wide open at me. They looked exactly the way I saw them in my dreams. So many nights I dreamed of this moment, and now it was finally here.

"Hi, Danielle," I finally said.

She lowered her hand from her mouth, allowing me to see her perfect smile. "Uh... c-come in!" She waved her arm and stepped to the side. I could feel her eyes on me as I brushed past her, wanting so badly to grab her, to embrace her immediately and never let go. Holding her after so long was like the first drink of water after almost dying of thirst in the desert. But I respected what felt appropriate. So much time had passed.

"Danielle, what time is it?" a voice came from the kitchen. "He's gonna be here any minute!" Michelle stepped into view, holding a cup of water in each hand.

"Hi, Michelle," I said with a smile and a wave. The two cups went crashing to the floor and Michelle burst into nervous laughter.

"Hi, Chris!" she said excitedly as she stood in place. She and Danielle looked at each other and back at me.

"Um, why don't you have a seat?" Danielle said. "I'll bring you a fresh cup of water. We'll make sure not to drop it this time."

Michelle squinted in offense at the tease. They seemed the same as they had always been, just older. Danielle motioned for her sister to join her in the kitchen. I had never seen either look that flustered before.

Quietly, I sat down, grateful to have a moment to pull myself together. I couldn't let them see me as the nervous wreck I was inside. I had to remind myself to breathe. Everything was riding on today. If this day didn't go well, my future could vanish; my destiny could change forever.

Muffled chatter came from the kitchen. It sounded like Danielle was panicking and Michelle was trying to calm her down. The sound of ice being disbursed into glasses obscured the voices. Then, silence fell upon the room.

I strained to listen, but a full minute passed without a sound. It spooked me until I noticed a picture frame on a shelf opposite the kitchen. In the glass I saw Danielle's reflection, standing at the kitchen doorway with a tray in her hands, her eyes closed, taking deep breaths.

Her nerves made me smile and calmed me down a bit. *Are you nervous about impressing me? If you only knew: there is nothing you could ever do that would make me stop loving you.*

The sound of the ice jingling in the glasses broke the silence. Danielle walked in and gave me a smile, setting the serving tray on the coffee table. She then sat down next to me on the couch, calm. She tucked her hair behind her ears nervously as she adjusted in the seat.

At last, there was nothing left to do but be together. We looked at each other. The energy between us was electric. The connection was still there.

"So, how are you?" she asked.

"I'm good," I said, clearing my throat. "Just moved into an apartment in Melbourne, so I'm in the midst of unpacking."

Her face lit up. "You live here now? Or... again?"

I nodded and smiled. Her cheeks lifted into the biggest smile I'd ever seen. "Well, things have changed a bit here since you left," she said.

"Not everything," I replied immediately with a grin. But her face dropped. The rejoinder seemed to catch her off guard. But as quickly as it left, her smile returned. She cleared her throat and pushed her hair behind her ears again.

"I'm sorry. I just can't get over how much *you've* changed," she said out of the blue. "You look amazing."

The girl of my dreams is sitting in front of me, and she's flirting with me! I wanted to pinch myself. "Well, you look even more beautiful than I could've imagined. And I've gotta be honest, I've imagined..."

We spent the next hour catching up, Danielle telling me all about her life. She tried to probe about my time in Michigan, but I revealed little, answering questions as vaguely as possible without being rude.

All that mattered to me for all those years was getting here, to this moment. But I couldn't just blurt that out. I would have to time it perfectly, eventually.

"Why so secretive about your life in Michigan?" she asked playfully. "I bet you had a lot of girlfriends, didn't you? Cheerleaders? The prom queen?"

I just laughed, "I did okay."

She laughed back and slapped me on the thigh. "You dog! You did, didn't you?"

We'd been shifting in our seats all this time, and by now our bodies were so close together that our knees were touching. We stared into each other's eyes as the conversation continued to flow. Every cell in my body ached to reach out and kiss her, but I didn't. I'd waited so long for the perfect moment, it felt like a waste to be impulsive now.

"So," she broke the pause, "let me get this straight. You're moving to Melbourne, right?"

"Moved, actually."

"Good! You'll need a tour guide! Have you been around town at all?" Her eyes lit up as I shook my head no. "I am at your service!" she said, making a little curtsy in her seat.

"Far be it from me to pass up such an invitation!" I said in a funny voice, joining in the silliness. I could hardly believe it; we were exactly as we'd always been.

"It's a date!" Then she looked away with a blush of embarrassment.

"I'm looking forward to it," I whispered softly, leaning in close. *More than you know.*

I leaned in and pulled her close to me, wrapping my arms completely around her. Finally.

"I want you to know how much I love you," I began. "I miss you so much. Dick took away your phone number, and I couldn't get it back. I was afraid you had moved on without me."

Her sweater was so soft against my skin. I could feel her chest rise and fall. This felt so right. We came apart just enough for her to study me.

"What happened to your jaw?" she asked softly, touching my face.

"My jaw?" I reached up to feel it, which made it pulsate. Why was it hurting? And then I was on the couch alone. The water in my glass started rising, overflowing onto the floor.

"Danielle? Danielle!"

Brack-brack-brack!

A screeching sound broke through the room, tearing its elements apart. The couch, the water, the feeling, it all vanished into black.

Brack-brack-brack!

NO! NO! Brack-brack-brack!

It was time for school. The bitter bite of a Michigan winter morning and the familiar loneliness of my existence sent a chill running through me as I rose to turn off the alarm. I sat on the edge of my bed and wept.

Just another morning in Michigan. I touched the pendant on my chest again. It was rusting. Its smooth edges changed until they were rough. Why else would God keep allowing her into my dreams if she were not my destiny? She was it: the end of generations of pain in my family, the mother of the future generations of my family who would make sure our past died with me. Despite the pain, I had to keep moving forward.

One day you will look back on this and tell your children how you won their mother back despite it all.

It was time for the final phase of the plan. With this next change, I would learn just how hard it is to be devoted when you finally have the thing you've always wanted.

1,648 days remaining...

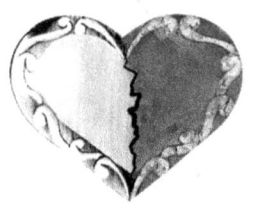

21

"Sharp Dressed Man"
(by ZZ Top)

My entire life shifted in my junior year of high school. Until that point, I never had to worry about the temptation to cheat. It could be, and to a degree, some argued I was in no position to cheat since I had moved out of state. Changes in geography resulted in a de facto breakup of young love, especially leaving as a thirteen-year-old. But my heart believed differently, and that was all that mattered to me.

Until that year, I had an advantage: girls weren't interested in me, so it was easy to keep my attention on the only one who ever was. As I entered my third year of high school, I was ready for the last big step in my master plan. I did not know that a much harder change would accompany it.

There was one small hair in the soup. I had to get permission from Mom and Dick, which felt almost impossible. Sometimes Dick didn't even let me finish my sentence before automatically shutting me down. There was never any reason for the denial, just "No," and, if he was feeling gregarious, "because I said so." He would walk away with a spring in his step, no doubt feeling proud for leaving me slack-jawed and angry. I couldn't wait to move out of that house.

So the evening that I sat them both down, I was prepared to fail. I made sure all of my chores were done, something Dick constantly harped on me about. I even did a few extra things around the house.

"Whatever it is, the answer is no," Dick quipped as they joined me at the kitchen table.

"Knock it off, Richard!" my mom snapped back. He grumbled under his breath as he plopped down in a seat.

Taking a calming breath, I tried looking at both of them for the first time with a hopeful optimism. Of all the times they shot me down, I really needed this one to stick. Surely no reasonable person would say no to someone trying to better themselves, right? But then again, my folks weren't always reasonable people.

But getting this done was a crucial part of my plan.

"I want to get contacts and change my hairstyle."

I waited for the verbal onslaught. Contacts were not cheap. Dick resented even paying for the food I ate, and Mom took over paying for karate after she found out Uncle Bob was paying for it.

"Absolutely not!" Dick snapped. But he fell silent as Mom held her hand up. I looked at her, stunned. Usually, she let him decide. But it appeared this time was different. She looked at me as if she was weighing her options.

I met her look, trying to get a read on what she was thinking. Was she seriously considering my request, or was she just trying to figure out a more creative way to say no?

"Okay."

She seemed to notice my sudden confusion.

"What? You're surprised?"

"YES!" Dick and I said in unison.

"He won't take care of them, hon!" Dick argued. The guy never gave me a chance. He gave a few more reasons I didn't deserve what I was asking for, and Mom nodded respectfully as he rattled on. When he ran out of air, she calmly continued.

"I still think he should get them. I think it would help him."

"Well, don't bitch at me after you spend the money and he loses them!" he roared, storming off into the kitchen to pout.

Mom let out a long sigh and looked down at the floor. After he was gone, she slowly looked back up at me.

"He has a point, Christopher. Contacts are expensive. And you aren't always the best at taking care of your things."

I couldn't believe Mom was on my side. Subtle insult aside, my shock jolted into excitement.

"I'll take good care of them, Mom. I promise!"

She rolled her eyes, but it felt affectionate.

"Really, Mom, I will!" I urged.

"I'll take you tomorrow," she said as she stood up. "Don't make me regret this."

She kept her word, and the next morning we went to the optometrist's office first and the pharmacy second to pick up the hair gel. It took some getting used to—touching your eyeball is a weird thing to do—but before long, I was ready to present the new me to the world.

My knees almost gave out when I saw myself in the mirror for the first time. I noticed the green in my eyes! It was like seeing a stranger in the mirror.

I'm good looking!

The Hydes couldn't keep their eyes off me, either. Aunt Bonnie loved my new look, as did Vicki and Katie. Even Michael gave me a thumbs-up.

Uncle Bob was beside himself.

"You sure you want to keep wearing that pendant?"

I looked at him, confused.

"You're gonna have to beat the girls off with a stick now!"

I dismissed what he was saying. Nothing was going to change. There was no way that hair gel and contacts were going to make that much of a difference. I would still be ignored, just like I had always been before. I was sure of that much.

• •

I could not have been more wrong. The next day I went to school with my hair gelled and green eyes exposed, and a brand-new letterman jacket, a bonus gift from Uncle Bob, to complete my new look. I loved the jacket. It was red with white leather sleeves and my name was on the bottom of the back along with "Coldwater" along the top.

As soon as I entered the building, it was as if I came in blaring a foghorn. The entire world seemed to come to a grinding halt as heads turned my direction. The stares felt like they were burning through me. They weren't negative stares. It was as if a new kid had arrived at the school.

To my amazement, girls were looking up as I passed. They were smiling at me! And these weren't half-hearted "You're sweet, but there's no way in hell I'd date you" smiles. These were the nervous smiles that Uncle Bob told me about, the flirty smiles that said, "You're cute." Some looked me up and down. I could still feel them eyeing me as I passed. Until then, I had never dreamt in my entire life that I would feel that kind of discomfort.

Each time a new set of eyes looked at me, my discomfort grew like a thorny vine within me, cutting deep as it went along. I was waiting for the first hand to rise and point, setting off a domino effect of laughter, but it never happened.

Finally, I made it to homeroom and slinked into my desk.

"Are you new here?" a girl named Nicole asked.

Seriously?

"We've been sitting next to each other in this class all year!" I answered, trying to contain my annoyance.

Her eyes almost bulged out of her head. "Oh my God! Chris? Is that you?"

I gave her my typical half smile and nod. I returned my attention back to the whispers buzzing around me.

"Wow... you look... like an entirely different person!"

Mr. Bailey actually walked into his desk when he saw me. He winced as he backed off, continuing to look at me as his arms reached out for his chair. I overheard the girls who'd talked to me after I read my poem whisper to each other.

"Did you see Chris?"

"Is that really him? That can't be him!"

I kept waiting for the other shoe to drop, but as time went on, my insecurities melted away. No one made fun of me. No one mocked me. Girls were noticing me for the right reasons, and it felt *amazing*.

Even the popular kids started talking to me. The guys who'd made fun of me suddenly stopped. They weren't completely friendly, but they were no longer cruel. They treated me like I was just another regular kid in class. For me, this was perfect.

My change was noticed outside of school as well. The first time I debuted my new look at the local music store, a couple of girls came near me while we thumbed through CDs. Then they came *really* close to me, something that had never happened before. They smiled and greeted me as I looked up. I couldn't believe what was happening!

"Do you like Nirvana?" one girl asked. As soon as she asked, her face turned bright red. "I mean, of course you must like it. You're looking at it!" she rambled nervously. She fussed with her hair as she tried to further explain her reasoning for the question.

I tried to be polite before walking away. *Do girls want to talk to me now?*

I had never felt so good about myself. The new Chris didn't just enter a room; he confidently glided. People I didn't know would smile and return my nod. Sometimes girls would just randomly start conversations with me. Sometimes they would give me a look of disappointment when I would politely excuse myself and leave.

I was a man reborn, coming forth from the abyss of aesthetic obscurity.

Then at a Sanchin-Ryu seminar, a gorgeous blonde from a couple of towns over developed a slight crush on me. We would drill and she would "accidentally" graze my groin when doing a downward strike, which must have been a favorite of hers because she did it constantly. I had never met someone who liked downward strikes so much. Every time she'd make contact, she'd grin like the Cheshire cat. When we parted ways, she apologized after "accidentally" smacking my ass. I could only watch her as she left.

Should I feel happy or violated?

I could feel yet another layer of confidence percolating. By this point, I had just gotten my third brown belt and was on my way to black. With my looks improved and my ability to defend myself increasing day by day, I felt an even stronger sense of determination in everything I did.

Even though I have a shaved head with a salt and pepper laced beard now (and some extra padding around the midsection), your dad still occasionally gets attention from women. Sometimes when we're out, your mom will suddenly start rubbing my back or randomly plant a kiss on the cheek. That's when I look around to spot a nearby woman looking on. I'd be lying if I said I didn't enjoy the attention, but it's all in good fun. Your dad is always faithful to your mom because I love her. I'm still the loyal man I always promised myself I would be.

Back in high school, though, it wasn't so easy. I went from being alone in devotion to a girl I hadn't seen in years to getting attention almost everywhere I went. My heart still belonged to the girl next door, but I was quickly becoming conflicted. I was quickly learning just how intoxicating female attention can be to a lonely heart.

1,048 days remaining...

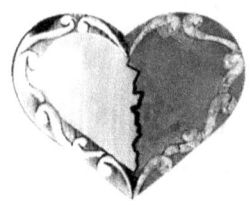

22

"Toy Soldiers"
(by Martika)

I'll never forget the day I met Amanda. It was 1995, and I'd recently started bowling at Midway Lanes on Saturdays. As a member of their junior bowling league, I'd finally made some real friends. Even though our team was all guys, the league was gender mixed.

One Saturday, we were playing against an all-girl team. Three of their players huddled together in the tables behind the lanes. Their fourth, a cute blonde, sat by herself in a chair farther up near the lanes. Over time, I couldn't help but notice they had completely isolated her from their group.

At first, she tried to smile when they sauntered past to bowl, their noses in the air. An hour later, she was near tears, trying desperately to not lose it. I watched as she quietly got up and disappeared into the bathroom.

Her time away cut into the flow of the game because her team had to wait for her when it was her turn. They clucked amongst themselves as they waited, pouting and grumbling about the delay. Just then, a black-haired woman who had been glaring at these mean girls bounded over to the ladies' room. She reemerged with the blonde in tow, her eyes all puffy.

She immediately went up to the lane and bowled her turn, her face turned down the whole time. She looked miserable, and my heart went out to her. I never understood how girls could be so nasty to each other.

One thing about your dad, he has a soft spot for women, especially those who are crying in front of him. I walked over to her exiled seat and pointed at the chair next to her.

"Is this seat taken?" I asked. She looked up at me, confused.

"I... I... No. You can sit."

I sat next to her and smiled. She glanced over at me periodically, an unsure look etched across her face.

"You're pretty good!" I said.

"Thanks," she said. "You're doing way better than me, though."

"Just luck," I shrugged. "I'm Chris."

She looked back at me again. I wasn't sure if I was freaking her out or not. She looked over at the woman who had fetched her from the bathroom before answering.

"Amanda."

Over the next hour, I chipped away at her defenses, cheering her on when she did well. As time passed, she relaxed and opened up. "And what about you?" she asked in the last frame. "Have you been bowling for a long time? Where do you go to school?" This was more than the basic attention I'd only just gotten used to. This girl seemed legitimately interested in who I was.

By the end of the game, we were laughing. Her teammates continued their whispers and nasty looks, even more upset because she started having a good time, but she ignored them. It felt great to be helpful to someone else who was obviously being bullied like I used to be. Even better that this someone was a girl!

After we packed up our bowling balls, Amanda walked me over to the woman with black hair and introduced her as her mother, Robin. Robin shook my hand and nudged her daughter. "See? I told you things would start looking up."

Amanda rolled her eyes.

"She doesn't enjoy admitting that her mom is right once in a while," Robin said, winking at me.

"Once in a while," Amanda quipped.

Robin shook her head and laughed. She reached into her purse and handed Amanda some money. "Why don't the two of you go next door and get some lunch? On me."

Amanda snatched the money and gave her mom a peck on the cheek. "Thanks, Mom."

We arrived at Wendy's and ordered a cheeseburger with fries and a milkshake each. Once the dust had settled from earlier, we went back to being awkward teenagers. She still seemed tense, as if something was really bothering her. She looked like she was ready to burst.

"What happened with your teammates back there? They really don't seem to like you," I asked, dipping a fry into my Frosty.

"Yeah," she said, her voice lowering a bit. She wiped her eyes quickly as tears developed.

"They stopped being my friends."

"Why?"

"I made a mistake. I mean... It's just... It's just a rumor!" She looked at me, pale and uncertain. I offered a smile to get her to relax. She returned it and sighed, her shoulders rolled forward, and her head bowed. She looked around and seemed to regret her revelation. Finally, she took a deep breath and looked me in the eyes.

"My boyfriend got me pregnant, and I got an abortion last week. Now everyone thinks I'm a slut."

I was not expecting anything like an abortion to come up in the conversation. I had to catch my drink before it spilled all over my lap.

"Oh," I started, taking a moment to collect myself and return my drink, "well, I know I just met you, but I don't think you're a slut. It sounds like... like you said. You just made a mistake."

Her eyes softened with a look of relief. I wasn't lying. That was what I honestly thought. I could tell just by looking at her she was a good person. It was as if I could see inside her, and I saw just someone like me, someone who just wanted to be accepted.

And so I told her my story, all the things I suffered because I was so ugly.

"Uh... you are not ugly *at all*," she retorted. "You're actually, like, great-looking. The girls were definitely checking you out, and they were so mad when you sat with me."

I just stared at her. Now I was the one about to lose it. "Thank you," I said, my face turning crimson. I cleared my throat and downed another chocolate-dipped fry.

We sat at that corner table for another hour, just talking about our lives. Turns out she was only thirteen years old, four years younger than me. Her seventeen-year-old boyfriend wanted nothing to do with a baby, but he was also very controlling. He insisted on the abortion.

Like me, Amanda was estranged from her father, which she believed led to a bad taste in boyfriends. After talking about everything else, at last I told her about Danielle. She listened intently, her eyes darting between my face and the pendant. The more I talked, the more her expression sank sorrowfully.

"She's lucky," Amanda said. "I know a million girls who would kill for a guy like you. We all want to be loved like that."

I was still having trouble getting used to compliments. Though I liked them, it felt weird.

Before long, Robin showed up. She sat with us and ate what was left of Amanda's fries. Amanda rolled her eyes and excused herself to the bathroom. Robin watched as her daughter disappeared.

"Thank you," she said.

"For what?"

"For being nice to her. Her friends can be real bitches sometimes." She lowered her head and whispered the curse.

I shook my head. "Of course, I'm nice to her. I've been that kid before, the one sitting alone. No one deserves that. And yeah, she seems great."

Robin smiled. "This may seem forward, but you're welcome to come over to our house and hang out if you like. Amanda needs more positive people in her life."

*

Amanda and I hung out often after that. No one else wanted to hang out with her, so I quickly became her go-to friend. We would see each other every weekend at bowling and soon outside of bowling as well. Since I didn't have my license yet, Robin would pick me up, or on rare occasions, my mother would drive me over to their house.

My mother didn't like me hanging out with a girl so much younger than me, especially one with her reputation. But, mostly because of that difference in age, I really didn't have any romantic inclination toward Amanda. I just wanted to show her what it was like to have a guy (albeit platonic) treat her with respect. My efforts to convince my mother of this were in vain.

Amanda's boyfriend didn't like me hanging out with her, either. The tension between us loomed over the house when I was over.

Eventually, they broke up. He blamed me, insisting she was screwing me behind his back. The problem was, even after they broke up, he refused to stay away. He'd creep by the house in his truck, trying to see inside the house. He'd call the house only to hang up if someone answered. As time passed, he became so obsessed that Robin took out a restraining order against him. Still, he kept appearing wherever she went.

Amanda's whole family tried to get him to leave her alone, but he refused. Every time they called the police, he disappeared. When she went to school, he would follow her between classes. Amanda denied being scared in the beginning, but as it ramped up, we could see it.

I wanted to stay out of the drama, especially since I'd only just met this family. But once I saw Amanda crying, it set me off. I was sick and tired of guys like this, guys who thought it was okay to terrorize women. He was just another version of my father, and all their efforts to stop him had failed. So, one day after he swung by, I followed him. The two of us had a friendly chat. I expand on what happened exactly, just that he promised to leave her alone after we concluded.

I returned to Amanda's a week later to find her and Robin happier than I had ever seen them.

"He's gone! We haven't seen him at all! It's like he just vanished!" Robin said as she went off to the kitchen.

Amanda stared me dead in the eyes as her mother floated off into the other room.

"Where did you go when you left last week?"

"I went out."

"Where?"

"Out."

Her hands were on her hips. She knew I was bullshitting.

"You did it, didn't you?"

"I don't know what you're talking about."

"Chris... What did you do to him?"

I cleared my throat. "I asked him to leave you alone."

By the way she looked at me, I knew she knew.

"He hasn't been at school."

I shuffled my feet, my hands in my pockets. "That's too bad."

She came closer to me. I kept my eye on her as she approached, waiting for her to hit me. Despite everything that had happened, she still loved him.

"Why did you do it?" she asked blankly. I looked her straight in the face and smiled.

"Because you are worth defending."

She suddenly threw her arms around my neck. The force of her hug was uncanny; I struggled to breathe. "Thank you," she sobbed as she held me in a vise grip.

From that point on, I was her guardian. Any problems she had with boys, she came to me for help. I'd inform them in the beginning of the relationship that I wasn't going anywhere, and I expected them to treat her with respect. All it took was one complaint from Amanda and the situation was dealt with... swiftly.

She had her share of boyfriends. All it took was one look from me and they kept in line. With each breakup, I was always there for her. With every breakup, she lamented on why she couldn't seem to pick a good guy.

After a few months, she took a break from dating. We continued spending time together, even cuddling together while we watched TV, but it was never romantic.

I was grateful to have someone to talk to about Danielle with. She was always willing to listen to me drone on about how much I missed her and how I planned to get her back. She would sometimes want to take a break from talking about the girl from Florida, but she was always willing to listen.

Since the famous poetry assignment, I'd started writing letters to Danielle, and sometimes I'd share what I wrote with Amanda. This was the straw that broke the camel's back. She usually listened carefully until one day she interrupted me with a terrible attitude.

"Why don't you just date someone?" she snapped. "I know people who would love to go out with you."

"It's not that simple," I stuttered. "You don't give up on the people you love."

"Yes, it is simple! Look, no one expects you to be faithful to her. You guys broke up. You're free!"

"We didn't break up!"

"You moved out of state. That's a breakup."

Until that point, I had refused to see it that way. But if Amanda saw it that way, maybe Danielle saw it that way as well. Had we broken up? Was she dating anyone else? Did she move on from me?

"You always look out for me," Amanda continued. "You're always so worried about me, telling me I deserve to be happy. Well, you deserve to be happy, too. What you're doing is so insanely romantic, but is it necessary? If she truly loves you, it won't matter if you date someone else before getting back to her. Do that for someone who is actually here!"

"Everyone knows I'm all about Danielle. Who do you think is so interested in dating me?"

"ME!" she growled in frustration.

It felt like a thousand-pound anvil dropped on my head. I thought of myself as her big brother.

"I know you keep telling me there are guys out there who will treat me the way I deserve, but I don't want them. I want you. You make me happy," she said, her tone softening. "You've made me happy since we met. My family loves you. It just makes sense! Don't you like me?"

My mind was racing. I didn't know what to say.

"I know how lonely you are," she went on. "You try to hide it, but I see you looking like you're about to cry every time you think no one's watching. You won't be lonely with me! If you give me a chance, I know I can make you forget all about Danielle. And if she really loved you, she would want you to be happy, anyway."

She got up and went over to my letterman jacket, which had been hanging on the back of one of her chairs. She picked it up and put it on. The sleeves ran over her wrists, her fingers barely showed. She admired herself in the mirror as I stared at her blankly.

"Just think about it," she said. "In the meantime, I'll wear your jacket."

She came over, kissed me on the cheek, and looked back before scampering downstairs.

The last thing I wanted to do was hurt her. Having the one good guy in her life break her heart could do some serious damage. She made some good points. Age difference aside, I could get some practice being a wonderful boyfriend, and she could see what it was like being treated well in a relationship. Didn't I deserve to be happy?

Still, a familiar voice echoed in my head.

Don't give up...

928 days remaining...

23

"Time"
(by Hans Zimmer)

Amanda's callout was fair. Six years had passed since we left Florida, and truth be told, I was losing it. As much as I tried to hide my moments of weakness, people close to me still noticed.

I avoided the circus at home by listening to music in my room all the time. Many of the songs I listened to reminded me of Fairhaven Street, and listening was the only way I could still feel close to her. But doing so only twisted the knife already lodged deep in my heart.

My mother yelled at me constantly to get out of my room and go do something. I began talking to Danielle in my room as if she were next to me. I'd have full conversations with her about everything in my life, the ups and the downs, wanting to know her opinion on things, begging her not to give up on me. Living in a house of thin walls, my behavior seemed to convince my mother that her son was losing his mind.

I wasn't crazy. I just missed my best friend.

Besides our "conversations," I wrote love letters, though I still had no address to send them to. I kept the growing pile of them hidden in a box under my bed.

These activities gave me some comfort, but the imagined sound of her voice did nothing to replace her touch. I craved the feel of her arms around me, the smell of her strawberried hair, the warmth of her body against mine, how it felt when she rubbed my back. I ached for the love and acceptance I only knew in her physical presence. Even though I'd improved myself, missing my love ate away at my insides.

Seeing other couples at school intensified my internal decay. Their happiness reminded me of what I would give anything to have again. My mind drifted into dangerous territory.

As time passed, I found myself second-guessing my plan, wondering if what I was doing was worth it. Then, one little thing would happen: a song on the radio, a sentence in a book or an episode of a TV show. It was always something simple that could pull me back from giving up. But with each rescue, it got harder to keep going.

I felt incomplete, like a part of me was missing and I was in a desperate search to find it. The only time in my life that I was ever truly happy was when I was with her. She was the missing piece to my puzzle—a maddening, gaping hole in the most beautiful picture of what my life could be.

I imagined our life together. My story was the grand gesture confessed to her right before proposing in Paris in front of the Eiffel Tower. We married at Cocoa Beach, Florida, right along the ocean, dancing for the first time to Survivor's "The Search Is Over" under the stars.

We had our difficulties. Sometimes we fought like crazy, but we always made up. We were a team and got through it all because we loved each other. There was no quitting with us because neither of us believed in divorce. We worked it out, no matter what. The pinnacle of our life together was our beautiful daughter, Emily.

Emily had her mother's looks, her brains, and my stubbornness. She was the only girl who could eclipse her mother's beauty in my eyes. Unlike the two of us, her eyes were a lighter shade of blue, though her hair was just as dark blonde as her mother's. Her giggle echoed throughout and brought life into our home.

As she grew, I taught her to defend herself. She loved martial arts and fought competitively. As I proudly put it, she didn't take shit from anyone - let alone boys. When she started dating, the "dad talk" happened to each boy. The talk was never for her, rather to protect the young man she was dating.

And she loved to hear about the story of how dad came back and won her mother's heart. She frequently asked us to tell it to her, though her mom was better at telling the story. Her chin would rest on her palm as she listened intently. She was a hopeless romantic, like her dad. As she would tell me before prom, my story gave her hope about men.

And my family loved me, no questions asked. There was never any judgment or condition attached to their love for me. I'd come home from work, a huge hug from my little girl and a kiss from my amazing wife. There was no screaming, no name calling, and no violence. I had finally ended the cycle of violence.

But it was all in my head, a figment of my imagination. It was the mirage on the desert path I was on to a future I was determined to believe was my destiny. All I had to do was endure the path I was on. My life was hard, but it was hard because the reward was so great. Nothing worthwhile ever comes easily. So, I continued to push forward.

Another strategy I used to help myself was distraction. Television was the easiest, helping me get through those days I counted down. I fell in love with the show *Friends* and saw myself and Danielle in the characters of Ross and Rachel.

Jennifer Aniston is a decent stand-in, I'd think, *but she's got nothing on Danielle.* I idealized their storybook relationship and took comfort in the hope it gave me—a reminder that anything was possible when two people really loved each other. If Ross could win back the love of his life after a long period apart, maybe I could, too.

Despite these efforts, I was slowly drowning. Day in and day out, I struggled against the riptide of reality, swimming with all my might toward the fading figure of my girl on the shore while I barely kept my head above water. Six years in, I was going under.

When Amanda came into my life, she gave me real companionship. While I balked at the idea of us being together as a couple, we started cuddling like a couple, and I liked it. It was nice having human contact. My mother would hug me occasionally, but it felt forced.

Amanda made a convincing argument. No one would blame me for dating. Some might even encourage it, saying it was a healthy exploration for a young man my age. Plus, it felt good knowing that someone cared about me, even if my parents couldn't stand her.

Still, the voice lingered in my head. *Don't give up.* This voice could reach me from a thousand miles away. It infiltrated every thought I had. Danielle still haunted my dreams most nights, reminders of what lay on the other side if only I just kept going.

And then Nicole came into my life as well.

• •

Nicole started talking to me right after my makeover. From that day forward, she made it a point to talk to me as much as she could. Whenever she would see me, she would light up.

Junior year, we had two classes together, homeroom and home economics. One day in Home Economics, Mrs. Albright broke the class into groups. Despite being assigned to a different group, Nicole defied the rules and shifted her desk next to mine.

"I'm with Chris!" she sang. Mrs. Albright looked over at me and rolled her eyes to turn her attention elsewhere.

I said nothing. I just looked at Nicole like she was crazy. Cute, but crazy. She was a sweet person, but I held it against her that she never noticed me when I was ugly. But as time went on, she grew on me. I would vent about my parents. She'd listen to me go on and on about becoming a lawyer, the first step in my plan to become a judge and watch as if I were the most fascinating guy alive.

I was rarely at home now. If I wasn't at Amanda's house, I was with Nicole. My life seemed to pick up, rebounding from the funk I was in. I had gone from being invisible to women to balance two great friends.

Nicole also listened to me talk about Danielle, though she would get annoyed and change the subject quickly. We started hanging out after school, sometimes at the park, sometimes going out for pizza or subs. She even came to watch me during karate class. She'd grin and cheer me on, remarking on how cute I looked in my *gi*. I remember Gary and Janice looking at me and mouthing, *who is she?*

"I just like to watch," she grinned from ear to ear when Gary invited her to join.

"Looks like she's got a crush," he said out of her earshot while grinning at me. I brushed him off, not sure if I wanted to believe it or not.

She even insisted on meeting my parents. I was shocked at how quickly she won them over. Even Dick liked her. He'd give her crap, and she'd give it right back to him. Mom enjoyed having another girl in the house.

"It's so obvious she likes you," Mom said.

"You're an idiot if you don't go out with her," Dick added.

Naturally, Nicole's inclusion into our family life led to another "one poor decision can ruin your life" speech from my mother.

I kept things platonic. Nicole made it increasingly obvious that she wanted more. She would make it a point to stand close to me, touching my arm here and there. This touching then turned to latching on, especially at school.

One day between classes, after Amanda detached from my arm, the girls who'd cheered me on after hearing my poem confronted me like a pack of hyenas.

"Are you and Nicole together?" one demanded.

"No," I shot back.

Their eyes passed secret messages between them. Finally, another girl broke the cold silence. "Don't be like other guys," she growled. "Danielle deserves better." She pointed a finger at me as they walked away. I could only watch in confusion as they flipped their hair and walked away.

What the hell?

I didn't know if they were jealous or if they were looking out for me. Why were they encouraging me to keep my promise to be faithful when so many were against it? Since that day in Mr. Bailey's class, I'd become an example of a good guy to them. For some of these girls, I was the only good guy their own age. If I broke my promise now, I wouldn't just let myself down.

The next day, as Nicole and I left our second class, she slipped a letter into my back pocket, asking me to read it later. Mrs. Albright raised an eyebrow as she witnessed the exchange.

When the lunch bell rang, I hung back outside the cafeteria to read it in private.

Dear Chris,

Over the last five months, I've started to really like you. I wish we got to know each other sooner because then we would have been able to have more time together. I love being with you and think you feel the same way.

I understand your feelings for Danielle and have tried to support you the best I can as a friend. But as your friend, I'm worried about you. I'm worried you're throwing away opportunities to be happy for someone who may not even love you anymore. I'm sorry if this breaks your heart, but I just don't want you to miss out on something great for something that may never be. Please don't be mad at me.

I like you as a friend and more. I've felt this way for a while. I know I can make you happy if you just give me a chance. Please don't be freaked out by this letter. I just want you to be happy.

Love,
Nicole

Looking up, I noticed Mrs. Albright over my shoulder. "That girl really likes you," she said. "If you value your friendship, be very mindful of how you respond."

The day after that, Nicole was visibly nervous, unusually quiet, and reserved. Eventually, we found some privacy and sat down to talk. She fidgeted with her hands and kept tucking her hair behind her ears. I had never seen a girl nervous to talk to me before. I wasn't sure how to proceed without hurting her.

"So? Did you read it?" she asked hopefully.

"I did."

"And?"

I took a deep breath before I spoke. "Thank you."

Nicole's eyebrows furrowed. "*Thanks?* That's all you have to say? I pour my heart out to you and all you have to say is *thanks*?"

"Wait. Hold on, look..." I held up my hands, but she rose to her feet.

"I can't believe I was *stupid* enough to tell you the truth."

"Hold on, Nicole!" I said, raising my voice. "Look, I'm screwed up in the head, okay? I'm not rejecting you, it's just... I don't even know what I feel! Part of me does like you, but I'm... conflicted. Can you give me some time? Please?"

"If you like me, why can't we be together? Why can't you just take that stupid necklace off? It's completely rusted! Why can't you just let her go?"

My entire body tensed, but I kept my mouth shut.

"And by the way," she demanded, "where is your letterman jacket?"

I felt like I had just gotten hit by a semi. I had not told Nicole about Amanda, or vice versa. At the time they were just my friends, or so I thought.

"A friend is borrowing it," I said nervously.

Her hands were now on her hips. "And who is this friend? Is it a girl?"

I blinked dumbly. Though we hadn't been talking long, talking to girls about my feelings was exhausting for me. My shoulders slumped.

"It *is* a girl!" Nicole's eyes grew weepy. She turned away, her shoulders slowly rising and falling. I could hear her sniffle as she furiously wiped her eyes with the sleeve of her shirt. I felt horrible as I watched.

But another part of me enjoyed the attention. It confirmed that I was no longer the ugly freak, unlikeable and unlovable. People cared about me. *Girls* cared about me. And it helped me feel less lonely. I was caught between my feelings for Nicole, Amanda, and Danielle.

"I feel like I've proven myself to you," she continued. "I'll give you some time, but the clock is ticking. You're still going on that trip to Paris with the school French Club, right?"

"Yes."

"I'll give you until you get back. If you don't have an answer for me by then, I'm gone." She walked up to me. Her anger seemed to lessen as she faced me. She leaned in and gently kissed me on the cheek.

"I'm worth it," she said, "but it's up to you to see that before it's too late. If I leave, I'm not coming back."

When I left her that night, I was desperate for a sign. I begged God for something to show undeniable proof that Danielle and I were meant to be and that my destiny was to return to her. It needed to be huge, something so big that it would leave no doubt in my mind.

Beware what you wish for...

900 days remaining...

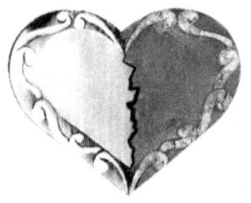

24

"Keep On Loving You"
(By REO Speedwagon)

Two weeks later, the Coldwater High School French Club arrived at Charles de Gaulle Airport at 9:48 a.m. amid a flurry of chaos. What we did not know that the media was going to jump us as soon as we exited the aircraft, or why.

It was just supposed to be a simple school trip: twelve students and three chaperones. Two weeks we were traveling with stops in England, Switzerland, Germany, and Italy, and a single day in Paris, paid for by generous parents. No doubt those same parents were scrambling for confirmation that their children were still alive once news got out about what happened.

Our French teacher, Mrs. Olsen, frantically pointed up at the arrival monitor as she conversed with one chaperone. The chaperone held her by the shoulders and motioned toward us. Another chaperone moved us to a room just outside the terminal where we could get away from the commotion. I watched Mrs. Olsen as we moved. Her hand was covering her mouth as she looked down.

"I have no clue what's going on," our chaperone said to a security guard. "All I know is we got off the plane, and these reporters tried to attack us!" The guard asked her to step outside for a moment.

It was then that Mrs. Olsen came back with the chaperone who had calmed her down. Behind them followed another woman with short black hair. Mrs. Olsen was still trying to collect herself.

The black-haired woman introduced herself as Tracy, our tour guide for the next two weeks. They sat Mrs. Olsen down as she sobbed into a tissue, the twelve of us looking at each other in confusion.

Tracy took over, leading us out of the main lobby. People all around us were crying and staring at television sets. One woman was frantically screaming as a man had his arm around her. As we passed the arrival board, I looked for the flight, bringing in a dozen students from another school that were supposed to join us here for the trip. It said *"Annule."*

Canceled.

That flight was TWA 800.

As we soon learned, that flight had exploded in midair twelve minutes after leaving New York's JFK Airport. There were no survivors. They were scheduled to arrive right after us.

Most haunting of all, I soon learned that we were originally booked to be on that flight. The school changed it to a direct flight out of Detroit at the last minute.

Within an hour, we'd arrived at our hotel. Exhausted, we checked in and went to our assigned rooms. It was suggested that we sleep off the jet lag, but I don't think any of us slept. I found myself alone in a room with two beds, the other for a child who was on that flight. The only english channel on the French television was CNN, which aired nothing but talk and photos of the crash and its victims. All I could do was watch as pictures of boys my age came onto the screen. I looked over at the other bed, wondering which one of those photos was supposed to be next to me.

A few hours later, we were called down to the hotel lobby. Tracy handed us updated itineraries for the rest of the trip. Everything had been changed because of someone leaking our itinerary to the press. We were told that our parents had been notified of the change.

This change included staying in Paris for the first day. I'd asked Mrs. Olsen prior to the trip if it would be possible to go to the Eiffel

Tower at night, wanting to live out the dream Danielle and I talked about as kids. I was still torn over what to do about Amanda and Nicole and I felt I might get some clarity if I could do something to feel closer to my first love again.

Mrs. Olsen said she didn't have a problem with my request as long as a chaperone accompanied me.

So, we toured Paris, the Arc de Triomphe, the Champs-Élysées, and Notre Dame. Before too long, night had fallen upon us, and I stared out the window of the restaurant we were having dinner in. The Eiffel Tower was in the distance and had yet to light up for the night. Once again, I asked Mrs. Olsen if I could go there after dinner.

"I don't know, Chris. Everyone is tired. I don't know if any of the adults will be up to taking you."

I was not happy. This was my one shot at doing it. I needed to go there. I *had* to go there. It was our dream, the Eiffel Tower at night. Just as I was about to protest, Tracy spoke up.

"I'll take him."

I wanted to run over and hug her. She'd chatted with me a few times throughout the day, and she seemed nice. She was in her twenties and reminded me of Courtney Cox. I smiled and thanked her, getting a wink back.

We separated from the group after dinner and trudged over to the landmark. The city was alive as we passed through side streets until we finally arrived. I cranked my neck back to look up at the tower as it looked over us.

"Why is this so important to you?" she asked as we approached the first elevators under the tower.

For the first time, I told an adult the full story of Danielle. Not even Uncle Bob knew the level of detail I unloaded onto Tracy. I guess I felt safe to speak because I knew I'd probably never see her again. She listened intently, taking in every word. By the time we made it to the top, she was visibly emotional.

"You know, I've just finished writing a novel based on a nasty breakup I had years ago," she said. "Writing it was one of the hardest things I had to do, but it was all worth it in the end. It helped me to finally move on with my life. I bet it would completely blow her mind if you wrote a book about all of this."

The elevator dinged as we reached the middle deck. Within moments, we were already in the last elevator to the top. As the doors opened and the top deck revealed itself, I hesitated.

I was finally here. My mind wandered back to when Danielle and I dreamed about this moment. I wished she was there with me. I could see her bouncing off the walls. In those moments, I felt connected to her again.

We made our way over to the ledge and looked out. I could see the vastness of the Parisian landscape. The city illuminated the air above it, giving it a slight warmth. The air was dry and a warm breeze lightly pushed against us.

At that moment, I stood exactly where we said we would one day stand together, so many years ago. Arriving at this very spot together would be the telltale sign we were finally adults. It would be proof that we were finally free to live our lives as we saw fit. It was the spot that I always saw as the sign that my new life had begun.

I lost it. I leaned on the banister, my shoulders heaving up and down, and quietly wept. Everything just came gushing out of me, the loneliness, the pain, the anger, everything. I was standing there, but without her. And I was still not free. This wasn't how it was supposed to be. Worst of all, from the time I had met Amanda and Nicole, I had become weak. I'd been seriously thinking about giving up on my destiny. Shame joined the other feelings pouring from me, shame for nearly succumbing to temptation. The pain of missing her was never more intense than it was in those moments.

"What's wrong?" Tracy asked as she lightly touched my shoulder.

"I just don't know what to do."

She rubbed my back as I pulled myself together. "Well, do you know what you want?"

I stopped to consider her question. The beliefs and expectations of those around me had convoluted the answer. I had been so focused on what other people wanted that I stopped listening to what I wanted. Now I wasn't even sure I could hear it.

"I don't know," I sobbed. "Am I wasting my time with Danielle?"

"I can only say this," she answered. "I imagine she would find it very difficult to say no after doing what you've done for her. But is it necessary to deny yourself now, before you can go back to her and ask for it? I don't know, Chris. It's not a simple decision, but no matter what you choose, any girl would be lucky to have you."

It was true. I was under no obligation to be faithful. If I saw other people, no one would judge me.

Amanda and Nicole were two amazing girls. I was attracted to each and for the first time in my love life, I had options. Both wanted me, *me* of all people. And they weren't the only ones. As I became more sensitive to the body language of women, I noticed interest more often. If I continued to wait for Danielle, I'd miss out on many of the experiences that defined high school for most people.

But most of all, if I dated other people, if I branched out and give others a chance, I wouldn't be lonely anymore. And I was so tired of being lonely. I didn't want to wake up in the middle of the night in tears anymore. I didn't want to look at other couples and feel envy and anger. I didn't want to suffer any more.

I was now almost nineteen and hadn't had a girlfriend in six years. Danielle wouldn't even have to know, and even if she did, I was sure she had dated other people. *She's gorgeous. Her options would be plentiful. She would be in no position to be upset.*

But I would know. I would know in that fateful moment when I told her everything, that earth-shattering announcement I'd imagined so many times turning her world upside down; it wouldn't be completely true. The sacrifice that I would claim to have made would be contaminated.

I needed to decide, not just about the girls, but about what kind of person I would choose to become. A promise breaker? A man who took the easy way out? A quitter?

Or did I want to be a man who saw his plans through to the end, no matter the outcome? A man who loved, endured and sacrificed for his one true love? A man who had proved his love by sacrificing the most important thing in life: time? Who would I be?

I'd prayed for direction, and I had gotten it. There, on the top of the Eiffel Tower, everything became so clear. God had saved me from being on that flight for this one reason: to win her back. Every single thing that had happened to me up to that point had prepared me for her, for the life we would have together. My parents and I could have moved anywhere in Palm Bay that year we arrived at Fairhaven Street, but we moved next door to Danielle. My life had been spared, so now I had a duty to see things through. There was no doubt in this direction, no convoluted flip-flopping. My choice was obvious, and it was this choice that stayed with me for years to come. I was ready to return to hell to earn my spot in heaven. My heart was hers and hers alone, and one day I would tell the story to my children.

We see this through, no matter the outcome.
Never give up on those you love.

728 days remaining...

25

"Life Must Go On"
(by Alter Bridge)

Nicole was gone. Her family moved to the Upper Peninsula of Michigan soon after I broke the news of my decision. She wouldn't even look at me when I told her.

Amanda stuck around, but I had broken her heart. Eventually she'd move on and forgive me, realizing that we were meant as brother and sister, and nothing more. She returned my letterman jacket.

Tensions with Dick were at an all-time high. As I grew older, our fights grew nastier, almost coming to blows occasionally. As I neared graduation, he pushed for me to leave, which led to fights with my mother.

And I was at a crossroads with Danielle. While my heart was permanently with her, the realization that our reunion was fast approaching exposed my insecurities. The time for my return was quickly approaching.

Despite my newfound confidence and colorful candy shell, I was still the same scared boy on the inside. I was petrified of rejection, not from others, but from her. I knew she wouldn't reject me for me, but what if she had met someone else? What if I was too late?

Another anxiety plagued me. I couldn't just show up with no money and no way to support myself. I needed a plan for what to do once I got back. I wasn't naïve enough to believe that I would get down on one knee as soon as I saw her. She deserved a good, old-fashioned courtship, nice and slow. I only had one shot to get it right.

Graduation was a few months away. I had no time to waste. The goal of leaving afterward was slowly dissolving into the realization that I needed more time. Love doesn't pay the bills.

My mother, true to form, sniffed out that I was planning on leaving after graduation.

"You'll be back. You'll end up homeless and come crawling back to me. Well, you've got another thing coming if you think I'm gonna drive down there to come get you. And then what do you think's gonna happen? All it takes is one poor decision to ruin your life."

With a heavy heart, I made my decision. Get to work full time and save. I'd waited almost seven years by that point; I could wait one more. My gut twisted, screaming that I was making a huge mistake, that the time to go was immediately after graduation, but my brain was firing back that it was too risky to show up with nothing to offer. I had to be smart about it.

Mom smirked contentedly when I told her of my new plan, though it brought Dick and I to the boiling point. I'd spent more than a decade living with his verbal and mental abuse, and it was about to come to an inevitable conclusion.

Mom was at work, and Dick had just returned home from a twelve-hour shift. I was lying down in my room, listening to music, when the headphones were suddenly yanked off my head.

"Can you make any more fucking noise, asshole? You know damn well I'm sleeping next door."

"I'm just standing here! I'm not making any noise."

"Yes, you are, you son of a bitch! I'm sick of your shit! You fucking freeloader! You should be out of here! Quit hiding under your mother's skirt and grow the hell up!"

Now I was getting a little hot under the collar.

"I told you," I said, standing my ground as he inched his face closer to mine, "I wasn't making any noise."

"Bullshit!"

His spit hit my face. I took a deep breath and looked him square in the eye.

"Look, believe whatever you want. I'm telling the truth."

His left hand went up in a fist. "You motherfucker!"

It all happened in slow motion. I could see the knuckles as they approached. This was it. He was going for a knockout. I had finally gone too far.

The surface under our feet shook violently as he crashed onto his left shoulder, his feet flipping over and smashing into my nearby dresser. Various items on top of it crashed to the wood floor below.

It all happened so fast. I just reacted. Good training will give that to a man. In one fluid motion, I intercepted his arm and threw him right over my shoulder.

He bellowed in pain, grasping at his shoulder as he rolled away from my dresser.

"YOU MOTHERFUCKER! YOU GODDAMN INGRATE!" He looked around, trying to piece together what had happened. "That's it! You are out of this house! GET OUT! Get your shit and leave!"

I knelt next to him. His bravado had changed to concern as I came close to him. He looked like he was barely holding it together.

"I'm not going anywhere," I said calmly. "And what if I did? Mom would want to know why. What would I tell her? That you came up and attacked me, like my father? She'd divorce you and leave you with nothing. No one fucks with her baby."

He snorted in pain as he pulled himself up against my dresser. We looked at each other, and in that moment, I could tell that the roles were reversing. This manly man, who my father had once backed down from, was just taken out by a skinny teenager.

"Don't touch me again," I said, walking out of the room.

That was the last time anyone ever bullied your dad. I ended up moving out anyway, into a house with a roommate ten minutes down the road. Despite my mother and her tears, it was time to move on.

*

Plans change. Sometimes more than once. Paying rent made saving a bigger challenge than I'd expected. I did the math, and what I was making wasn't enough to get me to Florida by the end of the year.

There was no way I could delay another year, so I needed a faster solution. I needed something that could give me enough income, but also allow me to move and have a steady job wherever I landed. I racked my brain for an answer. It didn't come to me until I spoke with one of my mentors, Judge David Coyle, former coach of the Coldwater High School Mock Trial team.

He told me he became a lawyer through the Army's Judge Advocate General's Corps. The military paid for his legal education and provided him with a job. While I wasn't too keen on joining the military, there was another branch of service that appealed to me. The United States Navy.

I spoke with a recruiter, who told me it was very possible to be stationed in Florida. He gave me all the information on how to make it into the JAG Corps and told me to think it over.

There was no way I was going to my parents with this. My mother would vehemently oppose it, that much I knew. I needed to talk to someone who had served before.

So, I went to Uncle Bob. He sat me down at the dinner table for a heart-to-heart.

"Why are you having doubts about the navy?" he asked, sipping his coffee.

"I don't know," I said sheepishly. "I've heard horror stories about basic training. Plus, I'm scared of the water."

He put his cup down, and the tone of the room shifted. "Christopher, I've known you for a long time now. I remember meeting this scared little boy at the hospital, too afraid to even look anyone in the eye. Despite everything your father did to him, I watched that boy grow up into a man. Hell, he even kicked Dick's ass!"

I looked down as he appeared to contemplate his next statement.

"Where is that man now?" he asked. "What happened to that confidence? You can do anything you put your mind to. Haven't you seen that by now?"

He took another sip of his coffee.

"If this is what you want to do, do it. Nothing is ever easy in this life. Go out and get what you want, because it will never be given to you. I love you like you're one of my sons, so I am going to say the same thing to you I would to them. Join. Quit being scared, get off your ass, and learn how to swim. Be the man I know you are."

Following that macho speech, the man choked up. "I don't want to see you leave, but leaving is part of growing up. Just know that I love you, son, and I'm damn proud of you."

He reached over with both arms and grabbed me in a viselike hug.

"I love you, kid. You'll do great."

Two days later, I went to the recruiter and signed. Janice, my friend from karate, agreed to teach me how to swim. She lived next to Coldwater Lake. Within three months, I could float at least. My entry was scheduled for six months from the time I joined, enough time for me to go back to Florida—with a plan.

• •

"WHAT?" My mother shrieked after I told her the news.

"I joined the Navy," I repeated. "I leave in January for basic training in Chicago."

"No you're not!" she hollered. By this time, Dick moved in close, but stayed silent.

"I am," I said. "I signed. I'm sorry, but I'm leaving."

Her mouth gaped open in shock. She suddenly shot in toward me, raising her arm up to slap me. Like with Dick, it all seemed to happen in slow motion.

Instead of throwing her, I caught her arm and held it in front of her. Her eyes suddenly widened in terror. She had tried to strike me. If I was going to prove all her fears that I'd turn out like my father, this was it.

I stared at her. It broke my heart how frightened she was.

"I'm leaving in January," I said calmly, gently lowering her arm and releasing it. "I love you, but it's done."

I looked over at Dick, who looked away.

"You are throwing your life away, Christopher," she said as the tears flowed. "The government will ruin your life!"

"It's my choice to make," I said.

And that was that. I'd proven to my mother and to myself that I was not like my father, or so I thought. Even thirty-plus years later, she's still not convinced that I'm not like him, even with your mom telling her I'm not. But back then, I'd soon have to prove it again when my father re-entered our lives.

That week, I received word that Grandma Leona, who had been living with my aunt Grace near Detroit for the last few years, was moving back to Florida. My aunt had been suffering her own health issues and could no longer take care of her.

I almost dropped the phone when she told me that my seventy-four-year-old grandmother was going to go live with the same man who almost beat my mother to death in front of me. The very person who had denied my father's abusive nature was about to have that theory tested. The problem was, no amount of denial changes how things actually are.

No one ever truly changes.

378 days remaining...

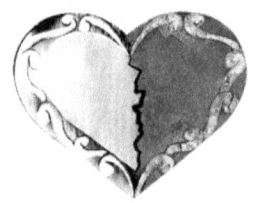

26

"I Grieve"
(by Peter Gabriel)

Six months later, my grandmother was flown back to Michigan and put in hospice. She weighed sixty-eight pounds when she returned, down from 112 when she first left to live with my father. It surprised the doctor she survived the flight.

As soon as I walked into her bedroom and saw her, I wanted to kill my father. I didn't want to hurt him, and I didn't want to beat him up. I wanted to take the life from his body when I saw what he did to her.

My heart felt like it was going to explode. I could hear it thundering in my head. I must have made some kind of sound, a shriek or a gasp because Aunt Grace's hand caressed my shoulder. My legs went numb, and I had to grab the doorknob to keep from falling down. I covered my mouth as I started bawling.

Even with her covers on, I could see how much weight she had lost. There was barely a bulge under her blanket. The only way to know there was a human being underneath were the shoulders and head that protruded out.

It got worse as I made my way closer to her. I fell to my knees next to her bed when her face came into view. It was almost completely hollowed out. Her eyes sunk into her occipital holes. Her face was gray, covered in pasty skin and devoid of muscle. She looked like a Halloween prop. The only sign of life was the light rasp of her breathing and the slight rise and fall of her abdomen.

The smell still haunts me to this day. There is no way to put into words the stench that emits from a person who is near death. It was a putrid odor that made me nauseous, the most revolting aroma of rot and bodily fluids.

Noticing some bruising on her hand, I reached over and slipped her right sleeve up. Her wheezing increased its tempo slightly.

A string of bruises marked the entire length of her arm. I knew those marks well; the kind caused by an object striking the skin, like a belt or strap. Tears streamed down my face as the picture of the end of her life came into focus.

She had only been with him for six months. My grandmother had survived breast cancer after a double mastectomy and had already started recovering when Aunt Grace said she couldn't take care of her anymore.

"Hi," she said weakly. She turned her head to me and attempted a smile. I reached over and held the back of her hand against my lips. I moved it to my cheek as she clicked her tongue. She perked up slightly as she looked at me.

"I'm okay, honey," she rasped slowly.

I tried my hardest to hold back the tears.

"What's wrong, C.J.?"

Ugh. That name. I looked over to the bookshelf near her bed and saw my father's picture staring back at me. His smug, leathery face with that stupid blond mustache and beady blue eyes. They took her out of that horrible house of his, yet he still loomed over her. Even my aunt's house wasn't safe.

"I go by Christopher now," I said. "I haven't been C.J. for years."

She looked at me, confused. "What happened to him?"

"Oh, I got rid of him with the rest of my past," I replied. "Tossed to the side of the interstate as we left Florida."

Her confusion turned to disappointment.

"Why did you do that, honey?"

"Because he was weak, a weak little boy!" I snapped back. The last thing I wanted was to yell at my grandma, but the emotion of the whole situation was getting the better of me. "Look at everything he let happen, the abuse, the bullying, the heartbreak!"

She swallowed with great effort and lifted her eyes to look back at me.

"C.J. is not gone."

"Yes, he is! Why do you keep calling me C.J.?"

"Because I still see him in you," she said. "You are still as much C.J. as you ever were. C.J. was a boy who fell in love."

"And look what happened. He left her!"

She coughed with great labor and tried to clear her throat.

"Only because he had to. He was a child. Oh honey, you'll always be C.J., no matter what you do. It's who you are. You can change your name, change your looks, you'll never get rid of him because he is your most pure heart, the absolute best of you. And C.J. is the boy Danielle fell in love with. I still see him here, as I'm sure she will soon."

I couldn't help it. Between the smell of the room and the stress of this conversation, I looked at my grandmother in disgust.

"How do you know that? What have I done to make you think I am still him? What have I done to make you think I'm weak?"

"Why do you think you're weak? Look at everything you've overcome in your life. You did it all for the love that C.J. helped you to find. Isn't that right?" her thin voice broke. "Love does not make a person weak, young man. It makes him stronger than he could ever imagine."

The fatigue in her voice provoked guilt in my heart. "You are more C.J. now than you have ever been."

I was desperately fighting back the tears by this point.

"But how can you say that, Grandma? Look at how much I've changed!" I barked, my voice breaking.

She slowly lifted her frail, trembling finger to point at the pendant. My breath left my body as she spoke.

"Because you never took that off. C.J. chose that pendant. C.J. asked me to help him be remembered by his first love. And when she sees you again, the memories that come rushing back to her will be her memories of C.J. Not this 'Christopher'."

She reached for me, and I held her hand. "Promise me something," she said. "Don't be like your father. I thought he'd changed. He swore to me he had. He was worse. I thanked God every day that you got away from him. Scott wasn't so lucky. Your dad found him homeless outside Melbourne Square Mall, begging for money. Drugs."

Her body heaved as her efforts to contain herself failed.

"Take care of your family when the time comes. Protect them."

I felt a frog in my throat as she finished. She was saying goodbye. She looked up at me, waiting for my response.

"I promise, Grandma. I promise."

She wrapped her fingers around my hand. "I love you, C.J. I always will."

At 3:28 a.m. that next morning, my grandmother drew her last breath.

• •

I didn't cry at her funeral. Even when they opened her casket for viewing, I remained stoic. The funeral home did as much as they could to make her look presentable. The blush they put on her face concealed the gray, but there was no way to hide the fact that she was just bones and skin. She wore a long-sleeved, powder blue blouse to hide her arms.

While everyone sat in the audience, I broke one chair away and pulled it next to the head of her coffin. I stayed next to her for two hours, nodding quietly to each person who came to pay their respects.

My eyes never left the double-door entry to the parlor. I was waiting, leaned forward in my foldout chair, my elbows resting on my knees, my fingers interlaced. My entire body was tense, like a coiled cobra, just waiting for my prey to enter. They said my father flew in the day prior to her service. He would be here soon, and I would wait for him.

Another painful thought crossed my mind as I sat there with my grandmother's coffin. Had he not cheated on her, my mother probably would've ended up the same way. Abusive people keep abusing as time goes on. The abuse only gets worse until they kill their victim.

And that's exactly what my grandmother was, a victim. She was a defenseless, elderly person who was completely at his mercy.

But my father never believed in mercy. He told us that several times.

There are people in this world who are pure evil. They cannot be reasoned with. There is no hope for their redemption. They do not make peace, nor do they love or care about you. They are cruel and malevolent and only stop their parade of terror when someone stronger makes them stop.

And that's what I planned to do when my father walked through that door.

In the days between her death and her service, more information emerged about what she had to endure in Florida. Most disturbing of all was the fact that she had a nurse visiting her regularly, yet nothing was reported. Florida wouldn't implement mandated reporting until seven years later in 2005. The one person who could have advocated for her did nothing. When interviewed, she said, "She was going to die soon, anyway."

These facts hammered away at my mind. My nostrils flared with every breath. I was popping both sets of knuckles furiously. Everyone who saw me wore an expression of nervous concern. I looked like I was getting ready to kill someone, because I was.

That changed my faith in people forever. Before, I had faith that people would ultimately do the right thing when it mattered most. Seeing my grandmother in that casket showed me that people will do what is in their own best interest. Filing a report was too inconvenient for the nurse. This severely intensified my desire to get into law.

Someone had to pay for what had happened to my grandmother. That left my father as the only candidate remaining. There would be no more courts, no more dialogue, no more second chances. Someone had to stop him before he hurt anyone else.

For so long, I'd followed the rules. Self-defense only. Ignore the bully and he'll leave you alone. Avoid violence at all costs. But those rules no longer applied to this monster or others like him. Violence was the only way.

The courts failed to stop him. Being civil failed. Leaving him to live his life only brought him back to me. And I knew he would keep coming back until he was gone.

He would see it coming, and I wanted him to. I could bait him to swing at me so I could destroy him. It wouldn't take much. I wanted him to suffer. And in the end, I would make sure he understood I was the one who did it to him. It would be the one time I would refer to myself as C.J.

And so I waited, eyes glued to the doors. My parents came over to check on me. I said nothing. Aunt Grace checked on me. I said nothing. I knew better. If I told anyone what I was thinking, they would try to stop me.

But after two hours, I overheard the news. Like a true coward, he had decided not to come after all, stating that he had "said his goodbye after dropping her off at the airport." In a few years, we would finally meet face-to-face. But that's a story for the next book.

He had dodged the bullet… for now.

I only left my post to give the eulogy. The service was beautiful. It was a packed house.

We buried Grandma at a small cemetery outside of Dundee, twenty of us holding hands and singing "Amazing Grace" as they lowered her into the ground.

As I threw a handful of soil onto her coffin, I touched the pendant under my dress shirt. I remembered our day at the mall. She gave me this gift because she believed in my love for the girl on Fairhaven Street. The last time we saw each other, she saw how scared I was. She could barely move or speak, but she had just enough in her to give her C.J. the push to fulfill his destiny.

It was time I stopped being scared about what may happen. I had enough money for a round-trip ticket to Florida and a rental car. I would go back and fight for Danielle if I had to. It was time for my new life to begin.

It was finally time to go home.

• •

The next day, I went over to Mom and Dick's. Mom asked me to stop off before heading back to my place, saying she'd packed up some stuff she thought I might want to keep. After small talk and hellos, I went upstairs to my old bedroom. When I opened the door, my heart stopped.

There, amongst my old things, were all the letters and poems I had written to Danielle, neatly organized on my bed. They had compromised my stash. My most intimate thoughts to her were now out.

Fine, I don't care. What's one more conversation about how I don't actually love her and how she's not worth what I'm doing for her? I'll remember that when I leave for Florida in the morning.

45 days remaining...

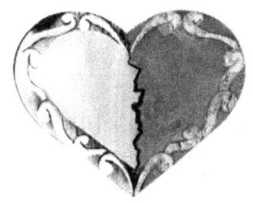

27

"(Everything I Do) I Do It for You"
(by Bryan Adams)

I was free.

I had finally reached the age where the shackles of my former life had fallen at my feet. I was free to go wherever I wanted, do whatever I wished, choose whatever direction I wanted my life to go in.

"Christopher, come downstairs, please. We want to talk to you about something."

No doubt the upcoming conversation with my parents was going to turn into another desperate attempt by my mother to convince me to not go to Florida.

I stood in front of my old bed, across from my old dresser. And I saw them as just that: *old* things. My former things that were no longer mine. This house, this family, this city, it had served its purpose. It had prepared me to get where I wanted to go.

As I slowly descended the stairs, I felt I had succeeded. This former ugly duckling who had quit everything he ever tried accomplished a truly remarkable thing. I became the man I wanted to become that day we crossed the Florida-Georgia line. I had remained faithful to the woman I loved for over seven years, not because I had to, but because I chose to.

I only needed to walk out of the door of this house one last time.

Just be polite and get out, I told myself as I cleared the last step. Outside the entrance to my parents' living room, I prepared myself mentally before entering. *Stay strong. The finish line is within sight.*

They were sitting in their respective recliners. I entered the room, determined. Nothing was going to deter me from leaving.

"Come, sit down, hon." My mother spoke with disarming gentleness. My shoulders were back and my head was high as I moved to the couch. I looked them both in the eyes, ready for whatever they had for me. This boy was no longer a child. I was a man.

"Dick and I've been talking," Mom continued. "We are taking one last trip down to Florida. Since you're leaving for the navy soon, we wanted to see if you would like to join us. We're going to lie low with one of Dick's old friends, so our car will be free—if you want to pay anyone a visit. We leave in two weeks."

She tilted her head with a little smile. I could see it in her eyes. She didn't say it, but she finally accepted that my love was real.

I had won.

• •

On December 13, 1998, my life in Coldwater came to an official close. It was time to say goodbye.

Uncle Bob did his best to stay strong. We spent the day together, he, Michael and I, just hanging out. He cooked his famous biscuits and gravy to send me off. He reminisced about me growing up in his house.

In the end, he grabbed me in a bear hug.

"Everyone else is proud of you, but not as much as me." A few tears hit my shoulder as he clutched me tighter. "I'm proud of you, son."

In a few short years, he would meet your mother and she would charm her way into his heart, too. I'll never forget when he nudged me when she stepped away. "I get what you saw in her."

Sensei Gary had a surprise for me before I left for Florida as well. When I went to my last karate class, I finally received my promotion to black belt. Gary presented it to me in the same gymnasium where I'd started out as an angry white belt in street clothes. Then, for the first time, he hugged me.

I also encountered the girls from school who'd pushed me to keep my promise to Danielle. They were shopping downtown when we ran into each other. The redhead shrieked when I told her I was leaving.

"You're going to go get her, aren't you?"

"Yes, I am."

The group of them mobbed me all at once.

"I knew you were a good guy!" one of them boasted, wiping her eyes.

We said our goodbyes and another of them yelled as I walked away. "Go get her and bring her back! We want to meet her!"

Amanda, or Aunt Amanda as it would pertain to the two of you, came over the night we were to leave for Florida. We sat on the porch and talked.

"So, tomorrow is the big day, right?"

"It is."

"You made it to the end. You did everything you said you were going to do."

She was right. No matter what happened next, tonight was a reason to celebrate. I'd earned it. I deserved to take a moment and recognize what I had done.

I could see that she was struggling to speak. Ever since I chose Danielle, she seemed sad when she was around me. She did her best to hide it, but I knew.

"Do you even know where she lives? Or if she's still in Florida?"

I took a moment and thought about it.

"Nope." I replied, shaking my head.

She raised her eyebrows. I could tell she wanted to say something, but seemed like she was holding back. "So, how are you going to find her? You won't be there very long, right?"

"Three days." I answered.

"That's going to be hard." She stood up and wrapped her arms around me. "But if anyone can do it, it's you."

She sniffled as she held me close. I then heard a soft whisper in my ear.

"Go get her."

She then handed me a card, left the porch, and walked over to her car. Opening the door, she stopped to look at me one last time. "Keep in touch, okay?"

I smiled and gave her a wave as her car sputtered to life.

As soon as she pulled away, I opened her card.

Dear Chris,

By now, I'm sure you're getting ready for the big trip to win the heart of your one true love. To be honest, I wish that person would have been me, but I see now that it was never meant to be.

You are the greatest guy I know, and I hope that when the time comes, Danielle is smart enough to realize what she has. You didn't mean to hurt me when you picked her. I should have seen it coming. I saw how you completely changed whenever her name came up. You were sad, yet happy at the same time. Your true self came out.

I was blind to this truth when I asked you out. I know now that you were always hers. No one else stood a chance. You are going to flip her world upside down when you tell her everything, just like you say. Just do me a favor and be patient with her, okay? It's like you've always told me: the best things in life are worth waiting for.

Know that I will always care about you. I will think of you often. Please bring Danielle to Coldwater when you get a chance. I want to meet her.

Love,
Amanda
P.S. You will always be my Danielle.

They would never meet. Amanda would eventually marry, and we would keep in touch only through Facebook. She would die in an apartment fire with her husband some years later. She loved keeping up with us, especially with updates regarding the two of you. I was her big brother right up to the end.

• •

The day finally came. I'd cleared out the room I'd been renting the week prior and now woke up in my old bedroom at Mom's. Like any other day, I got up and went to the dining room table with Dick. There were no snarky comments anymore. That changed the day I dumped him on his ass. It was our last day together in the old house on Pearl Street.

We packed the car like we had done so many years ago and set out to the state line. I watched as Coldwater disappeared behind us, as Palm Bay had done once before. My childhood was officially over.

No time for nostalgia. I had to focus.

How would I find her? I had three days to find one person in an entire state, possibly an entire country, with no phone number and no address. I had no idea where to begin. The phone book? We didn't have the technology back then to look someone up like we do now.

I wasn't giving up. Soon she would know everything. She would see me, and she would know. And if she was with another guy, so what? Whoever he was, his world was about to change. I hoped he had enjoyed his time with her, because it was never permanent. All he or any other guy could do was keep my spot warm. Soon, this minor detour of mine would be over with and I would be back where I belonged.

She was the person I was going to marry, not right away, but in time. That fact was as inevitable as the man I became. Danielle would be the mother of my children. Any man who might have her arm when I showed up would find himself unattached.

My feelings for her never waned, rather they grew stronger with every day that went by. We were torn from each other by the selfishness of others, but soon we would get back the time that was stolen from us. And I was going to do whatever it took to make it happen.

In the history of boy-wins-girl-back, I was no boy holding a boom box over my head. There was no field of her favorite flowers for me to stand in and beckon to her. There was no dream house to rebuild, so we could kiss in front of it in the rain.

I had no money, nor did I have a car. Instead, I had the greatest gesture of all: this story. All 2,740 days of it.

Now I just needed to find her.

2 days remaining...

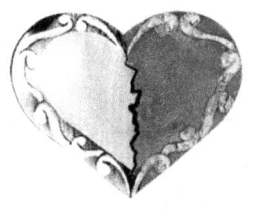

28

"This Year's Love"
(by David Gray)

We hit the Florida state line a day and a half later. As we passed the welcome sign, I couldn't help but look to the side of the opposing lane. The plants and greenery blurred as we thundered our way through.

My mind drifted to my grandmother's last words: that I was more C.J. than I had ever been. While it was still difficult to fathom the idea, I couldn't deny the truth about him being the boy Danielle fell in love with. He was also the one who became the man I now was. A pang of pity opened my heart as I realized I'd rejected him, just like everyone else.

Three hours later, we arrived at John Belcher's house in Palm Bay. John Belcher, or J.B., as my parents affectionately referred to him, had been a friend of Dick's for over thirty years. They worked together when Dick was a volunteer fire chief before he met my mother. J.B. had gotten to know me over the years and gave me the nickname Bubba, which I liked so much I passed it down to the two of you.

He welcomed us warmly, though I was so enveloped in my mission that I greeted him cold and quick. Dick objected.

"Sorry," I said quickly, "it's great to see you. Can I borrow your white pages?"

"Sure thing, Bubba. Right next to the phone. Make all the calls you need."

I bolted over to the phone as my mother began explaining what I was trying to do. Since the internet was just reaching popularity back then, the local white pages were the only way to look up someone's phone number and address.

I frantically turned through the pages, passing thousands of names. I needed a plan, and fast.

I started with her father's name, and I found twelve potential matches. It took me an hour to phone each one, but none knew who or what I was talking about.

Next were the twenty-five potential matches for Danielle. Some were home, some weren't and required a callback. I kept a detailed list to track who I'd need to try again. About an hour and a half into my calls, J.B. came to check on me.

"How ya doin', Bubba? You've been on the phone a while."

I rubbed my temples, lamenting failure number twenty-two.

"Been better," I said. "Sorry, I'm monopolizing your phone."

He lightly slapped me on the back. "Don't worry about it. I've been in your shoes before. Keep going. You'll find her."

All twenty-five were a bust. I was panicking, but I still had one last option.

There were thirty-eight women in the area who had the same name as her mother. My neck was cramping from holding the phone so my hands could take notes.

I tried to remain optimistic but grew increasingly frustrated as I neared the end of the list with still no success. If none of them were listed in the Palm Bay white pages, I'd have to find a phone booth in Melbourne and try those. If Melbourne didn't work, I'd just keep chewing through every local phone book in south Florida.

Number twenty-three was a ninety-year-old woman who screamed at me. Twenty-four was a married mother of one who gave me a lecture on how rude cold calls were. I crossed her off my list and stared down at the last number.

My sweaty fingers slipped off the buttons as I dialed.

God, if this was meant to be, let this be it.

The receiver rang in my ear, and my heart pounded in my chest. A click later, a woman's voice picked up. "Hello?"

"Hello. I was wondering if you could help me. I'm looking for a woman who was mother to two daughters named Danielle and Michelle and lived on Fairhaven Street in Palm Bay some years ago."

"Um... yes. That's me. Who, may I ask, is calling?"

My mind was racing. I found her! I had to quickly collect my thoughts, so she didn't hang up.

"It's Chris. I used to live next door to you guys. How's it going?"

A long pause made her side silent.

"I'm... wow! Oh, hi, Chris! My gosh, it's been a long time! How are you?"

"I'm good," I said, thanking God under my breath. "I'm in town for a few days from Michigan."

I crossed my fingers and asked the same question I had rehearsed so many times before when I dreamt of our reunion.

"Hey, is Danielle there by chance?"

Another long pause.

"Um... no, she's not, Chris. I'm sorry. She's on leave right now. She joined the Navy about a year or so ago and lives in Japan now."

My heart would have hit the floor if it hadn't been in my body. She wasn't in Florida. She wasn't even in the country.

Okay, she may not be here, but let's at least go see her family. My inner voice came to the rescue with a plan. *We can find out exactly where in Japan she's stationed.*

"Okay," I said, trying to hide my disappointment. "That's okay."

"Okay, well, it's good to hear from you."

"Wait!" I exclaimed, catching her before she hung up. "Is it okay if I come over and see you guys, anyway? Maybe you could give me her address."

She took a deep breath. "Okay. Sure. How about tomorrow? Eleven a.m.?"

"Great. I'll be there."

"Look forward to it."

I took down her address and hung up. This wasn't how the plan was supposed to go. She was supposed to be there, and we were supposed to reunite! Still, it was better than not finding them at all. I tore the paper with her number and address and tucked it deep into my wallet. Then I wrote them down again and put this second paper in the pocket of my suitcase.

J.B. and my folks stared at me, looking for an update.

"Looks like I'm going to Japan."

• •

I turned off J.B.'s van and stared out the windshield. Danielle's parents' new house was small and sat at the end of a long gravel driveway that connected to the street between two long rows of trees. They stood tall, blocking passing traffic from seeing through.

Rosebushes adorned the sides of the walkway to the front door, but there were no roses on them this time of year. Two steps up, a spacious porch held up the rest of the little house. A scrub jay called his lonely call.

I opened the van door and hopped out. *This is not how it's supposed to be. She's supposed to be behind that door.* I had dreamt it so many times that I couldn't believe reality could turn out differently.

The point seemed moot as I stopped to look at myself in the side mirror. I looked good, the only similarity to the dreams. I stared at my reflection, noting how far I had come in becoming who I was. Still, the irony stung… all that work and she wasn't even there to see it.

Walking up to the porch, I could imagine Danielle bounding out the front door to go to school every day. I could see her humming in the rocking chairs that sat on each side of the front door or talking to her friends on the phone. I couldn't help but wonder if she sat there and thought about me as well.

I had missed so much of her life. But even with all the disappointment of this empty arrival, I couldn't help but be proud of how far I had come. The journey would just be longer than expected. I would go to Japan if she was there. If she was in Russia, that's where I would go. If she was in Antarctica, that's where I would go. No matter where she went, I would follow until I found her. There was no one left to stand in our way.

So, I stepped up and rang the doorbell.

"HANG ON!"

I recognized that yell immediately. Her mom still sounded the same. I waited patiently, my hands in my pockets, seeing shadows move behind the curtains. With a resounding *click*, the doorknob turned and the door opened.

A loud gasp suddenly came out of the house. Then a woman's voice, different from the one I'd just heard, called out to me.

"Oh my God... Chris? Is that you?"

My whole body went numb. The woman moved forward, breaching the threshold.

It was Danielle.

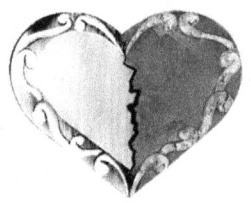

29

"At Last"
(by Etta James)

Everything that lived and breathed came to a screeching halt, stopped still, with all of time, at 11:00 a.m. on December 15, 1998. The scrub jays ceased their serenade, and the Floridian winds held their position while a man and a woman who had once loved each other faced one another again for the first time in almost eight years. And it felt like the first time all over again.

Destiny had been fulfilled. Despite all the obstacles and tragedies that a lesser man would've let defeat him, I had arrived at my destination, the only place I'd ever wanted to be, reunited with my one true love.

Her mouth hung open. Her eyes widened, those enchanting emeralds scanning me from top to bottom. Then her hand darted out, grasping the doorframe to keep steady.

I had the opposite problem: I couldn't move. I was glued to the wooden boards beneath my feet. My legs refused to cooperate; the unexpected turn of events shocked my nervous system. I knew I needed to say something, but my brain was as stuck as my feet. It wasn't until I heard the sweetest sound to fall upon my ears in a long time that I finally came to.

"Hi," she said.

My ears trembled at the sound of her voice, my brain still in doubt if this was real. But that single word sent a chill vibrating down my spine. I'd dreamt of that sound for so long, thirsted desperately to have it fall upon my ears once again. It was the sound of salvation.

"Hi!" I blurted out, forcing myself forward.

Dark blonde hair hung around her shoulders like a curtain of silk, each strand perfectly straight at the end. A wisp of it fell just next to her eye, which she swiftly swept back into place.

Though her freckles had faded, I could still make them out. Her button nose was now well in proportion with her face. Her cheeks were fuller, still tinged with red. And her smile warmed my heart, a sweetness that put me at ease, with a playfulness that told me we were about to have some fun.

"Um, come on in!" she said energetically.

I was mesmerized as she led me inside. She had an elegance about her, a maturity that drew me in. Her shoulders back, she carried herself with a confidence that made my knees weak. She didn't simply walk across a room; she glided like the angel she was. The awkwardness of her childhood had melted away and left a sophisticated woman emerging from its wake.

And what a woman she was, through and through. I couldn't help but let my eyes inspect her from top to bottom as I followed. She moved with subtle sensuality, showing just enough of her grown-up curves to get my attention. Every move had a fluid grace to it.

"Was that him, Danielle?" Her mom asked as she emerged from the kitchen. She abruptly halted as soon as she saw me. Her eyes were almost as big as Danielle's in those first moments after seeing me.

"Oh wow," she said, uncomfortably looking at her daughter. "You really grew up, Chris!"

"Definitely!" Danielle agreed, raising an eyebrow.

Her mom stood in front of us awkwardly, and we all struggled with what to say next.

"Chris, why don't you have a seat here on the couch with me? Mom, could you bring us some water, please?"

I sat, surprised by the formality with which she now spoke, amazed by how much she had grown up.

She joined me on the couch, and her mother disappeared. She cleared her throat and tucked her hair behind her ears. Uncle Bob warned me about that move. A good sign.

The connection was immediate, as if we had seen each other only yesterday. I could hear my heart in my chest. My palms were moist. I had finished wiping them on my pants discreetly when I was stopped in my tracks by a sensation I'd not felt in years.

Butterflies.

My world was spinning. Everything was happening so fast. I desperately tried to keep myself under control. Almost eight years, and she was now sitting next to me like she had done so many times before.

Her mom returned with two full cups on a tray. She placed them in front of us and smiled.

"Let me know if you guys need anything else."

Danielle smiled in appreciation as she excused herself back into the kitchen.

"So, I have to ask right off the bat," she said as she put her cup down on the coffee table in front of us. "When did all of *this* happen?" she laughed, waving her hand over my body.

I smiled. "A few years ago."

She seemed almost entranced as she rested her chin on her palm.

"Well, I just can't get over how you look. You look incredible."

She reached over and took a drink.

"You must have been popular with the girls, I bet."

My face turned crimson.

"I got some attention."

"I bet! So, is there anyone special in your life right now?"

She went right for it! A good sign!

I could only chuckle and clear my throat uncomfortably. Every fiber of my being wanted to just tell her everything. My story needed to be heard; it smashed repeatedly at the door of my throat, screaming to escape, yet I continued to restrain myself. Now was not the time to confess my undying love to her.

I found my hand sneaking toward her, between us, on the couch. I willfully brought it to my lap and held it with the other. But to my surprise, she took the initiative and put her hand on mine, albeit for a moment. I almost jumped at the feel of her warmth. I was having a hard time breathing. Her touch was intoxicating, and I craved more.

Deep down, I knew it was too soon. I needed to be patient. Still, the way she moved closer to me, turned so that our knees were touching, her elbow on top of the couch, her hand in hair. It all said *Speak! Take your shot!*

But I continued to restrain myself. She was everything I ever dreamed of and more. I couldn't blow my chances with an overeager revelation. It took every ounce of resolve to hold myself back from telling all.

As she talked about her life, our life together flashed before my eyes. The images I had memorized for years came and went, following one another other like an old film.

Even when Danielle took out a scrapbook, my mind continued its slideshow of future memories. I saw myself carry her over the threshold of our first house. We were kissing under the mistletoe and wearing ugly Christmas sweaters. I saw her showing me a positive pregnancy test and the two of us hugging. I put my head on her very pregnant belly, listening to our baby kick.

And then I saw six-year-old Emily sitting next to us on the couch with her legs crossed at the ankles, her hands in her lap. She gave me the sweetest smile to cheer me on. She had not been created yet, and I was already in love with her.

Then I snapped back to the scrapbook. Danielle pointed to a group photo from her senior prom, enthusiastically waving her hands as she shared a story about that night. My heart melted as she laughed at my jokes. A sense of peace washed over me, like I was finally where I belonged. For the first time in a long time, I was truly happy, like I was on Fairhaven Street.

And then, in one glorious moment, she suddenly let out a loud belch.

"Danielle!" her mom yelled from the kitchen. Danielle held her hand over her mouth in embarrassment. But it seemed more like she was trying not to laugh.

"I am so sorry," she said, putting her hand down, a sly smile appearing on her face.

I fell in love with her all over again. My Danielle.

"Wait!" she said excitedly. "You said you joined the Navy, right?"

"Yeah."

Her face lit up.

"Me, too! I joined almost two years ago! Hey, I'm transferring to Norfolk in a couple of months. When you get out of basic, I'll tell you where I am, and you can move out there!"

A huge smile spread across my face. I had done it. My faith was being rewarded. She wanted us to be in each other's lives again. God knows I'd move to Norfolk in a second. I was already prepared to move to Japan for her. My excitement mounted and I nearly burst with it, shouting, "I've waited for you all these years!"

But I didn't. It was still too soon. If I couldn't tell her everything yet, there was one thing I could do: pull the necklace out. If I showed it to her, no doubt she would put two and two together. I imagined the look on her face as she did the math and waited for her to stop talking for a moment so I could push the conversation in that direction. Just as I was about to do it, her mom appeared in front of us.

"Sorry to interrupt you guys," she said, "but they're here, Danielle."

"What? Oh yeah. Sorry." She smiled at me and put her hand on mine again before getting up. "I'll be right back!"

She dashed away from me and out the front door. Her mom gave me an awkward smile as the two of us waited. I pulled the pendant from beneath my shirt and let it hang down. When I looked up, I saw a horrified look on her mom's face. She looked at me, at the necklace, and then back at me again.

Before she could say anything, Danielle came back in the front door with two other women and a chubby older man in tow. He had a scruffy beard, a short spiked haircut and a smirk on his face. He saw me and cleared his throat.

Danielle introduced me to the ladies first. They were both friends of hers from high school. I stood and shook their hands. They smiled and made small talk for a few moments before being whisked away by her mom.

I waited to see if she would notice the pendant. Her eyes darted back and forth between her friends and I as she spoke. She seemed completely oblivious to the tarnished piece of steel that now hung from my neck. If I could just get her to notice it, she would know everything, and the stage would be set for the beginning of our new life together.

But she was going a mile a minute.

Just look down! I screamed in my head each time she looked at me. *It's just a few inches! Look down, Danielle!*

But she didn't. Once her friends left the room, she immediately turned her attention back to the man who had followed them in.

"Chris, this is Steve." She squeezed his arm and held on. "My fiancé."

30

"Someone You Loved"
(By Lewis Capaldi)

From the outside, I'm sure I looked calm, but on the inside, I was panicking. My gut was twisting. Everything I'd sacrificed, everything I'd dreamed of, all hung before me by a thread. I was prepared for a boyfriend, maybe even a long-term boyfriend, but a fiancé?

Neither of us offered a hand to shake when she introduced us. Though he had walked in happy and jovial as soon as he laid eyes on me, his expression turned stiff and serious.

The three of us went into the dining room and sat, Steve and I facing each other at the far ends of the table, Danielle on one side, chattering on about how she and Steve were supposed to have gone to lunch, but she stayed behind because of my visit.

Mid-sentence, mid-syllable, she stopped. Her face had gone completely blank as she stared at my chest. The hook was in.

"Danielle?" Steve asked. She just stared at me, completely ignoring him. Her eyes alternated between the pendant and my face.

"So, how do you guys know each other again?" Steve asked. Danielle's eyes remained locked. She sniffled and her fiancé looked at her.

"Chris is the first guy I ever loved," she answered softly, her mouth curling into a smile.

I KNEW IT! Every single person who said she didn't care about you anymore was wrong. I was right! I always knew it!

Steve shifted in his seat and cleared his throat.

Now is the time! TELL HER!

"Best three years of my life," I said.

Danielle clicked her tongue.

"Me, too."

You need to fight for her, Chris!

"Remember the tire swing next to your old house?"

"I do," she laughed. "I also remember you almost killing me on it!"

"I had you. I always kept you safe."

She let out a long, contemplative sigh.

"There was one other memory from that swing I'll never forget..."

"Our first kiss!" she interrupted excitedly. Steve was now drumming his fingers on the table. He looked over at her mom, who had poked her head out from the kitchen, then returned his attention forward, glaring at me.

I would not give up. Obviously, this was not the scared little boy they thought was coming. I knew this was making things worse. I didn't care. She was my future, and I was going to win, no matter what I had to do.

I also felt the possibility of physical violence in this situation. I scanned the room in preparation. He'd probably approach from the side of the table opposite Danielle, near the bookcase. Using his size, he would probably try to knock me into the furniture, just like Dick. He'd never see it coming, never guess I was a black belt in karate. Danielle would never hold it against me because I'd never hit him.

Let him attack you, so she'll see how unhinged he is. I hoped it would happen that way.

"So, I, uh, hear you're going to Great Lakes for boot camp soon," Steve said.

"Yep."

"Well, boot camp is really hard. Hopefully, you'll make it."

"I've survived worse," I replied, looking at Danielle. "Inspiration helps."

He had now interlaced his fingers together so tightly that his knuckles were white. My turn.

"And when did the two of you meet?" I asked.

"Like a year and a half ago, right, babe?" Steve reached over and started rubbing her back.

"Wow. Long time," I said dryly.

A year and a half ago... that's right after you graduated! I told you to stick to the plan!

"I told Chris to get orders out to Norfolk where we're going so he can live near us. He can come over every weekend," she smiled.

Steven cleared his throat loudly. "Well, not *every* weekend."

A look of disappointment spread across Danielle's face. She shrugged it off and leaned over toward me, looking at the pendant.

"What is that? Half a heart?" Steve's tone reminded me of the boys in high school.

"I used to have one just like it," Danielle said. "Why is it tarnished, Chris?"

Steve scoffed. "Didn't believe in cleaning it, huh?"

"Actually," I said, holding it between my index finger and thumb, "I never took it off."

"What," Danielle jolted. "It's been what, almost eight years? You never took that off in all that time?"

"Not one time. It almost got torn off in my karate class, but luckily, it stayed on."

Danielle plopped back down in her seat like it had knocked her back. Her eyebrows knit together.

My plan was working. Lead in with subtlety and finish with the emotional nuke.

But Steve's voice interrupted her thoughts. "Danielle, can I talk with you for a minute? Alone?"

She snapped out of her trance and nodded. "Sure." They disappeared into a nearby bedroom, Danielle looking at me, stunned, as they walked over.

From where I sat, I could only hear the muffled sounds of conversation in the room. The longer they were in there, the more uncomfortable I got. I knew what he was doing. He was taking a stand.

He wasn't stupid. His fiancée was slipping away before his eyes. He was probably giving her a big speech, maybe even an ultimatum.

Now is the time. When they come back out, just tell her everything. You can't afford to keep this close to the chest anymore.

It was time. I had waited eight long years for this moment, when I'd tell the love of my life all that I'd done for her. All I would ask of her was one date, just one. That's all I needed, and Steve would be gone. Destiny was about to be fulfilled.

But a smaller voice whispered behind these thoughts. *Loving someone means putting their happiness ahead of your own.*

Bullshit. I argued back. *She's happy with me. We just need more time to reconnect. The two of us were always meant to be together. I moved into that house on Fairhaven because we were destined to be together. This guy is just a footnote. I deserve this! I earned this!*

Suddenly, I felt ashamed. Was this about love, or about me getting what I felt I deserved? Did I love her, or did I just love the idea of her? Is it loving to interrupt her life plans and pull the rug out from under her? Was I only here to take what I believed rightly belonged to me? Was collecting my trophy more important than whether she was happy?

My father treated my mother like a possession, meant to follow his script, to do what he decided was best. I knew that was no way to love someone, and I didn't want to be that way. I also saw my mother's influence on my behavior. Her obsession with winning, with getting what she felt she deserved, indifferent to how this taking affected others, was now showing through me.

And what did this say about who I'd become? All these years, the guiding light for my evolution was to be the man Danielle deserved. But did the man she deserved care more about his own feelings than hers?

STOP RIGHT NOW. If you don't do this, you are going to destroy everything you've worked for. Your future will be gone. The last eight years will have been for nothing. She still loves you! Drop the nuke and END THIS!

I looked over at the couch. Emily was smiling at me again, only now she was a teenager.

"Dad? Tell me the story of how you won mom back!"

The click of the door opening shook me from my internal conflict. Eight long, grueling years boiled down to what I was about to say. Standing up, I moved to the side of the table as they stood before me. Steven glared at me with his arms crossed, his scarlet, rotund face slightly concealing a tense jaw.

The decision was final. I was taking my shot.

"Danielle, I need to tell you something..."

• •

But I stopped talking when I saw her face. Her eyes were red and puffy. She crossed her arms in front as she clutched her elbows. Her eyes fixated on the heavily tarnished pendant around my neck. She was forlorn, her cheeks swollen and damp.

I'd made her cry when I swore to myself I wouldn't. I remembered my mother crying on the phone so many years ago. It was that fateful day that I learned then how disloyalty could destroy a person. The love of my life was suffering, and I was the cause. I was no different from my father.

Danielle would never forsake her fiancé. She was a loyal person. To tempt her to break that loyalty would go against everything I stood for and turn her against me. Sure, she was loyal to me, once upon a time. But my time had passed. She had chosen him. Despite the walk down memory lane, she'd moved on from me, and it was all my fault for not sticking with the plan. All I could do from here was cause her pain, like the pain I saw on her face before me. The woman I loved was miserable, but this time I could do something about it.

I tapped the table with my fist in frustration.

"Chris," she said softly. "Do you have something you want to say?"

Steve rolled his eyes.

Every single muscle in my body ached. I felt like I was ten years old again. I looked up at her, my mouth opening to speak. Part of me held on… if anyone deserved a chance, it was me.

But I said nothing.

I wanted to scream about how unfair this all was. This wasn't the way things were supposed to be! I had earned a chance! If anyone ever in the history of men had ever been more deserving of a chance with a woman, it was me! But those thoughts were selfish. Acting on them was something my father would do. And I was not my father. And as I've told you boys many times before, life isn't fair.

I decided that the man I had pushed so hard to become, the man who deserved Danielle, would let her live her life in peace. He would do the one thing my father and mother refused to do in life. He would lose, willingly. I had changed for her, and now I would destroy my world for her.

I looked over at the couch again to see it was empty. Emily was no more.

Steve beamed, triumphant, as I stood there in quiet tension.

"It's time for you to go," he trumpeted, breaking the silence.

Danielle stopped him as he went for the door. "I'll escort him out."

With a heavy sigh, I followed. The family I had longed to be part of for so long had already filled my place with a man she had only known for only a year and a half. I was still not worthy of joining their ranks.

We walked out past the roseless rosebushes, out to the street, stopping just shy of the van. Time had caught up to us, the man and woman who were supposed to be, but couldn't.

Danielle then made a gesture that broke my heart. She offered to shake my hand.

This was the end of it all. I could see the film of our future burning, one scene at a time. The world I had spent eight years creating was falling apart around me, gathering as rubble around my feet. Everything I had been through, everything I had sacrificed, was summed up by a platonic hand extended to me by the one person I was never supposed to lose. My simple request for just one date was denied without even getting a chance to ask for it.

My limbs felt numb, my head fuzzy. The only feeling in my body was the very sharp pain that cut across my heart. My life was over before it even began.

"Can we hug?" I asked.

Remorsefully, she said, "Of course."

She came in, and for one last, exquisite moment, I held her close to me. I'd dreamed a thousand restless nights of the warmth of her body, and it was everything I'd remembered and more. It took every ounce of my remaining resolve to not lose control of my emotions. I could feel tears run down my cheeks and slowly drip onto the back of her shoulder as we embraced. The dagger deepened into my heart as the scent of her hair filled my nose.

Strawberries.

When it came down to her happiness versus mine, hers was more important, even if it destroyed me. Keeping my mouth shut and leaving seemed the only way I could prove my love once and for all, and she would never even know I'd done it.

We slowly parted, and I reluctantly started the van. I drove away. She watched me go, staying in place until I had pulled out of sight onto the main road.

My Danielle was gone. She and Steven would be married in a courtroom a week later.

I needed some music, something to soften the blow. "Dust in the Wind" by Kansas came on when I turned on the radio. I would've preferred Queen's "Love of My Life," but this was before the age of the iPod. I didn't even bring any CDs with me. As I listened, I heard my new fate.

Tears broke through as my vision blurred. I pulled the van to the side of the road and let it idle as the song echoed in my mind.

Other motorists zipped by. The van lurched as each one passed. My arms rested on the steering wheel; my head came down upon them as the song continued to drill itself into my mind. The crack in my heart quaked open deeper. My inner voice, the voice that had for years pushed me toward this moment, had now turned on me.

All you had to do was stick to the plan. You've just made the biggest mistake of your life! This will follow you like a shadow until the day you die.

I looked up to see the sun disappearing behind the trees in the distance. Nightfall had come upon the rubble of my life.

I failed.

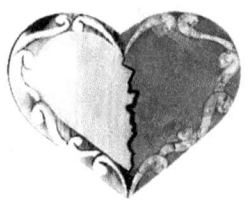

EPILOGUE

"Goodbye Yellow Brick Road"
(by Elton John)

A man's heart isn't supposed to break, or so the rule is according to society. He is expected to never let the world know that he is in pain. I can tell you boys from personal experience that a man's heart breaks just as easily as a woman's, though it can be argued that we suffer more because of the restrictions on our ability to deal with it. But as you get older, I want you both to know there is no shame in having a broken heart, nor is there any in expressing the pain you feel from it. Allowing yourself to feel emotion doesn't make you any less of a man.

For fifteen years, I stepped back and watched Danielle from afar via Facebook, not wanting to complicate her life because of her husband's reaction. We would speak occasionally; she was always quick to reply on Messenger. Our friendship existed with a self-imposed caveat that I not reveal my true feelings for her since we were both married to different people. We would send sweet birthday messages to each other, and she was always eager to know more about how the two of you were doing. I still referred to her as my best friend, telling her on more than one occasion that meeting her was one of the best things that ever happened to me.

There are few things in life that are more painful than loving someone and not being able to express it to them. Having to see them with someone else while not being able to tell them of this amazing thing you did for them was torment. Logic would dictate that keeping in touch with her for as long as I did was unhealthy. But my options were simple: tell her and possibly complicate the friendship we did have or keep the secret, suffer in silence but keep her in my life, albeit in a limited capacity. It may not have been healthy, but it was the closest I could ever be to having her in my life again.

But it was a long journey from 1998 to now.

We lost touch for over eight years after 1998 before connecting on Facebook. In that time, I struggled with what happened that day during my time in the Navy. The book I had planned to write to her was pushed back in the recesses of my mind to never see the light of day. Amanda repeatedly pushed me to find her and tell her everything, but I refused. The pain I felt was both physical and emotional, and every day that pain grew by a small amount. I still dreamt of her, being reminded constantly of the life I missed because I didn't listen to my gut. Broken Heart Syndrome is very real.

I grew to believe I would never feel the warmth and acceptance that I had dreamt of years earlier, and with every day that went by, that fate became more and more apparent. And it was my fault. The thing that had kept me going for so long was now slowly killing me from the inside.

I made the mistake one time of telling some of my co-workers about her. Suddenly, I was no longer a man because I was stupid enough to do what I did for her. The only way to rectify the problem was to bed as many women as I could, or so they told me. I took them up on it and while it was surprisingly easy, I was miserable the whole time.

I quickly learned that no number of one-night stands would ever change the fact that I had lost Danielle. After years of trying, I decided I would be alone for the rest of my life, not because I felt sorry for myself, but because I didn't want anyone else. I became obsessed with making plans and seeing them through, no matter what.

I was addicted to accomplishment, and as time passed, I began working later and later every day. I would snap at people for the smallest things. I was a loner, frequently spending time by myself rather than socializing with others. I was unforgiving and cold. People would ask me why I never smiled. I never told them what was wrong. Truth was, I was trying to fill a hole that could never be filled. As unrealistic as it was, deep down there was always that hope that one day, somehow, the stars would align, and we would reunite and eventually be together.

My pain worsened until I caught myself wishing I had never met her. So, one day, I tried to pretend she never existed in the first place. This backfired and sent me into an emotional tailspin. Eventually the realization hit that I was never going to be with her. This was the final straw which led to a plan to kill myself. After five years of trying to move forward, I had failed. If I couldn't be with the one person who ever truly loved me, then I didn't want to live anymore. It was too painful. I told no one because I knew they would try to stop me. It took a random encounter with a celebrity while on a flight from Atlanta to Tokyo at the eleventh hour to change my course. God had reminded me that He existed yet again, though I had turned from Him because, in my mind, He had betrayed me.

I began going to counseling after that point. Over the years various counselors tried to explain how my feelings were wrong and abnormal via logic and science. Apparently, I had somehow conditioned myself to feeling depression and heartbreak. Love can never be explained with logic, and I had experienced the truest of love in a relationship which had ended without resolution. This meant the feelings I had were never going away.

Eventually I found a counselor with a different approach. It was through this person that I realized that I was not wrong for feeling what I did, but I had to change my mindset if I was to ever move forward with my life. The only way to move forward was to recognize my role in everything that happened to me rather than feel sorry for myself. I had developed the same victim mentality that my parents had. No one made me do what I did for Danielle. I chose that path willingly, knowing full well the risks involved. Sometimes, even when you do everything right and have earned another chance, the answer is still no.

This mindset applied to everything else that had ever happened to me. What I quickly learned was that mindset gave me the control I had always wanted in my life. Taking responsibility for the things that happened in your life is frightening, but self-accountability allows us to grow and change. Blaming others for our plight in life gives away all our power. We can learn from and change what happens to us in life by recognizing that we contributed to it.

My counselor suggested I date so long as I no longer use Danielle to reject women. I deserved to be happy, and, despite my belief, it was possible to be happy with someone else.

It was then that I met your mother. We met at an IHOP of all places. As we dated, I realized there was a connection between us, and there was a real possibility of it turning into something serious. So, I tested the relationship. I told her about Danielle on our second date and waited to see where the chips fell. I honestly thought she would leave.

I told her everything. I also told her that if she wanted to be in a relationship with me, she would have to understand that Danielle wasn't going away. I was ready to let another into my heart, but Danielle had her own permanent spot first. If that was too much, we could part ways with no hurt feelings.

Your mother stayed. She stood by my side as I continued my journey with counseling. I slowly made peace with everything else in my past. The devotion I had to making sure Danielle never experienced abuse shifted to your mom. Your mom became the first woman in over a hundred years to not be abused by a male member of our family.

We married and started our new life together. Your Nana and Papa on your mom's side welcomed me into their large, close-knit family with open arms. I went into the marriage with a great deal of guilt because the feelings I had for the girl from Fairhaven Street were still there. Marrying your mom caused my heart to become two halves: one half was the husband. It was spotless, pristine, a shiny part of my existence. That half was endless love for her, representing a deep devotion to my marriage and to the life we had together. It would never leave or forsake her.

The other half was tarnished and beat up. It had been run through the ringer, but it was still going strong. This was Danielle.

Throughout our marriage, I have tried to be as transparent as possible with her about everything to do with the girl from Fairhaven Street. The goal was to make sure she never had reason to doubt what I told her. Your mom knew I was still talking to her and had full access to our conversations. Understandably so, your mom wasn't always comfortable with the situation, so I did my best to be sensitive to her feelings. I explained that if Danielle were to show up on my front door and express her undying love for me, asking me to be with her instead, my answer would be no. It would be the most painful thing I ever had to do, but the answer would not change. I'm fully confident that will never happen because I know Danielle. She's the most loyal person I've ever known.

In 2017, your mom and I were blessed with not one but two sons at the same time. Over time I watched the two of you grow up. Before I knew it, I was coming home from work and being welcomed by a warm hug around my waist by little arms and a kiss with a nice backrub from my wife on a regular basis. I got to hear those amazing words of "I love you, daddy" before tucking both of you in at night. Right now, you two worship the ground I walk on, and I'm enjoying it while I can.

But I have been blind to the blessings I have. What I had failed to realize over time was that the life I had always wanted…I already had. I was wanted. I was accepted, but most of all, I was finally loved unconditionally. I have a large family now who cares about me. Writing this book made me realize this. While this beautiful epiphany brought warmth to my heart, the complications that came from the tarnished side remained.

Regardless of my continued devotion to my marriage, society still does not approve of a man loving someone in addition to his spouse, and I have been subject to concern and ridicule on quite a few occasions. Boys, never allow anyone to make you feel shame for loving someone like I have. I am not a bad person, nor am I a bad husband, and I have tried hard over the years to give your mom the best life I can.

But I have allowed myself to be locked up in my own emotional prison of shame because I made the mistake of caring more about what other people thought of me than what was in my heart.

The shame I allowed myself to feel had taken its toll not only on me, but on the two of you and your mom as well. I became prone to depression, which affected my ability to be the father and husband I needed to be. It took Amanda's sudden death to wake me up to the harsh truth that life is too short to be harboring secrets. People will have their opinions, and that's okay. No matter what happens or who I lose as friends, my feelings will never change. My counselor's advice at this point was simple: it was time to write the book that would eventually be known as Destiny Lives on Fairhaven Street.

This book made me realize that the only way to free myself from my emotional prison was to take how I felt and own it… and finally tell Danielle the truth. What had begun as the grandest of gestures became so much more. It was time to tell my truth.

I still love Danielle. I've loved her for thirty-five years, and I will love her for thirty-five more. After so many years, the promise I made to her before moving away is still alive within me. The photos I have on my computer at work as well as my office have photos of your mom and I, photos of us as a family, of you guys, and of Danielle.

Her photos have picked me up from the darkest of times in my life. I see her and I'm reminded of who I am. I'm reminded that there is NOTHING in this world that I cannot do. Her photos got me through the four years of hell that it took to write this book as well as the 138 rejections I had to endure before finally getting it published. It has won numerous awards and every single win, every single accolade it earns past, present and future, is dedicated to the girl from Fairhaven Street.

We have gone our separate ways over the years, and yes, we have changed. But I believe deep underneath all those adult layers of change, Danielle and I are still the same kids from Fairhaven Street who still love each other. I offer no apologies for the way I feel. When it comes to my feelings for the love of my life, she was worth the ridicule back then, and she's still worth it today.

I love your mom more than she will ever know. Her love and support are also a massive reason I am the man I am today. I've loved her for 17 years and I will love her for 35 more as well. God has blessed me with two of the most amazing women He ever created, and I'm a better man for it. Both Danielle and your mom deserve to know how important they are to me.

This is why this book is only the first of a series I have titled "The Fairhaven Series." This book was for Danielle, the next will be for your mom. Book two will tell the story of my travels across the world in the Navy, meeting your mom and the push for us to have children. It features various celebrities I've had the pleasure of encountering in my life such as Britney Spears, Jessica Biel and Ted Dibiase.

I realize now that my destiny never resided in a person, rather it was for me to end the cycle of abuse so the two of you, as well as future generations, could ensure it never returns. Our painful past dies with me, as it should be. It is up to the two of you to forge a new future for our family. I have complete faith that you will make me proud. I will always love the two of you with all my heart. By the end of this series, the both of you will finally know what I have been saying since your birth… the two of you were meant to be.

And in closing the story of my childhood, the truth has broken my shackles. I see now more than ever that I've had an amazing life. I have loved. I have lost. I love again.

My name is C.J. Hudson, and I am finally free.

About the Author

As a child, C.J. Hudson became inspired to write when he fell in love with the girl next door. Theirs was a whirlwind romance over three years that ended when they were forced apart by his abusive family. His journey back to her would become the bases of his multi-award-winning romantic memoir debut, *Destiny Lives on Fairhaven Street*. Though he looks like he belongs on a harley rather than behind a keyboard, Mr. Hudson enjoys the result of his literary journey in the form of twin boys and a loving wife in Pflugerville, Texas. And he still doesn't own a harley...yet.

Note from C.J. Hudson

Word-of-mouth is crucial for any author to succeed. If you enjoyed *Destiny Lives on Fairhaven Street*, please leave a review online—anywhere you are able. Even if it's just a sentence or two. It would make all the difference and would be very much appreciated.

Thanks!
C.J. Hudson

We hope you enjoyed reading this title from:

www.blackrosewriting.com

Subscribe to our mailing list – *The Rosevine* – and receive **FREE** books, daily deals, and stay current with news about upcoming
releases and our hottest authors.
Scan the QR code below to sign up.

Already a subscriber? Please accept a sincere thank you for being a fan of Black Rose Writing authors.

View other Black Rose Writing titles at
www.blackrosewriting.com/books and use promo code
PRINT to receive a **20% discount** when purchasing.

www.ingramcontent.com/pod-product-compliance
Lightning Source LLC
Chambersburg PA
CBHW071959070526
44583CB00015B/1251